D1393967

CONTENTS

941. 83 DUND

Items should be returned on or before the last date shown below. Items not already requested by other borrowers may be renewed in person, in writing or by telephone. To renew, please quote the number on the barcode label. To renew online a PIN is required. This can be requested at your local library.
Renew online @ **www.dublincitypubliclibraries.ie**
Fines charged for overdue items will include postage incurred in recovery. Damage to or loss of items will be charged to the borrower.

THE
LITTLE
BOOK
OF
DUNDRUM

HUGH ORAM

The
History
Press
Ireland

First published 2014

The History Press Ireland
50 City Quay
Dublin 2
Ireland
www.thehistorypress.ie

© Hugh Oram, 2014

British Library Cataloguing in Publication Data.
A catalogue record for this book is available from the British Library.

ISBN 978 1 84588 846 6

Typesetting and origination by The History Press

ACKNOWLEDGEMENTS

Firstly, I'd like to thank my wife Bernadette for her patience and understanding while I was compiling and writing this book. As always, she has been an unerring guide along the journey. I'd like give especial thanks to Jacqueline Holohan, for her drawings used in the book; Grants, Upper Baggot Street, Dublin 4, for all their help with the images (Grant Howie and Martin McElroy) and Dean Lochner of the Bondi Group, Dublin 2, for his computing assistance. William O'Brien, senior assistant librarian in Dundrum Library; the staff of Pembroke Library, Anglesea Road, Dublin 4; Berni Metcalfe of the National Library of Ireland; John G. Lennon, Dundrum & District Historical Society; Kevin Harrington, Dundrum, author of *The Way to Dundrum* (1988). Don Nugent, Jeanette Jordan (usually known simply as JJ) and Aideen Moran, all of Dundrum Town Centre; Pat Lafferty, Lafferty Associates, Dundrum; Irene McGrane, Orla Hanratty and Grainne Millar at Airfield; Shan Kelly, Windy Arbour Village Association; Pat Herbert and Joe Guilfoyle, Ye Olde Hurdy Gurdy Wireless Museum, Howth; Catherine KilBride (Mount Anville); Ronan Lee, Dundrum; Tony and Paddy Collins (Uncle Tom's Cabin); Paddy Ryan (Ryan's Dundrum House and Ryan's Windy Arbour); Peter Cassidy (Dropping Well); Frank Mulvey, Mulvey's Pharmacy, Dundrum); Peter Pearson, County Wexford, for permission to use photographs and a map from his book, *Between the Mountains and the Sea* (O'Brien Press, Dublin, 1998); Ultan Mac Mathúna, principal, Holy Cross National School, Dundrum; Tony Dempsey, of Roughan & O'Donovan, Sandyford, design engineers for the Dargan Luas bridge in Dundrum and Councillor Pat Hand, Dundrum; Tom Byrne, executive secretary of the Ten Pin Bowling Association; James Burns, general manager, Milltown Golf Club. John Lowe (moneydoctor.ie); Dave Downey (Dublin Book Browsers, Stillorgan); Bronagh Moore (Irish Management Institute); Fr Donal

McCarthy, Pallotine Fathers, Sandyford; Roly Saul of the eponymous restaurant in Dundrum; Brenda O'Beirne, Holy Cross parish office, Dundrum; Patricia Mellon, Broadway, County Wexford; Ciáran Cooney, honorary photographic archivist, Irish Railway Records Society, Dublin; Pauline Kent, marketing officer, Dundrum Credit Union; Oran O'Rua, Balally Players; Dún Laoghaire-Rathdown County Council communications office; Myra McPartlin, Mill Theatre, Dundrum Town Centre; Ken Mawhinney, An Taisce; Russell Bryce (Fianna Fáil headquarters) and Sara Scally, DMOD architects, Dublin, designers of Taney Parish Centre.

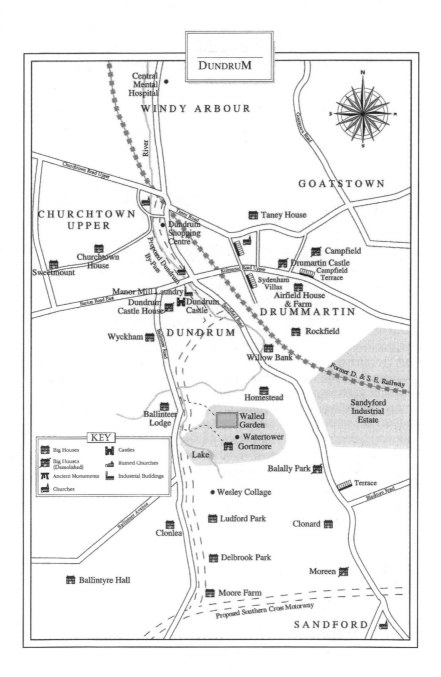

1

TIMELINE

Seventh century	The original St Nahi's (St Nasi's) church is built. Frequent raids into what is now the Dundrum area by Wicklow tribes, including the O'Byrnes and the O'Tooles; these continue until the sixteenth century.
1178	First mention of Tawney or Taney parish.
1179	Papal Bull mentions 'the middle place of Tighney'.
Twelfth century	Soon after the Anglo-Norman conquest of Ireland in 1169, the lands at Dundrum and Taney were assigned to the de Clahull family. However, their tenure lasts less than a century.
1268	The lands at Dundrum come into the possession of Sir Robert Baggot of Baggotrath.
Thirteenth century	The original Dundrum Castle is built close to the site of the present Holy Cross Catholic church; the name Dundrum comes from the Irish for 'fort on the ridge'. The castle had been built to keep the Wicklow tribes at bay.
Fourteenth century	In the earlier part of this century, Ireland was in a state of lawlessness and the lands between Dundrum and Dublin were completely devastated. The Fitzwilliams, who came from around Swords, take control of the lands in the Dundrum area.
1593	New version of Dundrum Castle is built by Richard Fitzwilliam.
1640	The Dundrum population included thirty-three Catholics and fourteen Protestants.

1653	The last of the Fitzwilliam family to have lived in Dundrum Castle, William, had departed, although they retained control until the late eighteenth century.
1730	Mill House, in its present form, was built, although some reports say it was built earlier.
1791	Earliest surviving original records of Taney parish.
1801	Dundrum has an iron mill and a paper mill, both on the River Slang.
1813	Original Catholic church is built on Main Street.
1818	Present Taney Church of Ireland church is built.
1850	Central Criminal Lunatic Asylum is opened at Windy Arbour.
1853	Queen Victoria visits William Dargan, Ireland's great railway builder, at his home, Mount Anville.
1854	The Dublin and South Eastern Railway, later known as the Harcourt Street line, arrives in Dundrum. The railway station opens on 10 July 1854.
1856	Dundrum Courthouse is built.
1866	Extensions to Mount Anville as the present school opens in the former house of William Dargan.
1878	Holy Cross church opens in Dundrum and the parish created the following year.
1892	Dundrum is recorded as having a population of 540; the village consists of little more than the main street.
1894	Trevor Overend, a Dublin solicitor, buys an eighteenth-century farmhouse at Balally, which after reconstruction, became Airfield.
1901	Census: Farranboley (Windy Arbour) had twenty-six houses.
1903	Dun Emer Press, in which W.B. Yeats and some of his family were closely involved, opened in Dundrum.
1907	King Edward VII and Queen Alexandra visit the races at Leopardstown, returning to Dublin via Balally and Dundrum, bedecked in Union Jack flags for the occasion.
1911	Census: Dundrum has 140 houses.
1912	During the visit to Ireland of King George V and Queen Mary, they visited Leopardstown Races.

Coming back from the racecourse, the route included Dundrum's Main Street, festooned for the occasion with Union Jack flags, as in 1907.

1914 Carnegie Library opens in Dundrum.

1917 A local GP, Dr Isaac Usher, is knocked down and killed by a car near the railway station and an obelisk with a fountain is later erected nearby in his memory.

1921 On 11 July 1921 a truce is declared, bringing the War of Independence to an end. A celebratory bonfire is lit at the crossroads in Dundrum that evening.

1923	On 24 May the Civil War, which had begun in June 1922, ends. Many of the negotiations to end it had been conducted in the Dundrum area.
1942	Manor Mill Laundry closes down after trading for nearly eighty years.
1943	Pye opens its radio factory in Dundrum, making wireless sets and similar appliances; in its heyday it was the largest employer in the area.
1959	1 January the Harcourt Street line, including Dundrum railway station, closes down.
1969	Dom Marmian Society opens to help the disabled, the old, the sick and the lonely in Dundrum.
1971	Dundrum Shopping Centre, one of the earliest in Ireland, opens on Main Street in Dundrum. It's now known as the Dundrum Village Centre.
1981	Jim Nolan publishes the first edition of his book, *The Changing Face of Dundrum*. It went through five editions to 1993.
1990	Dún Laoghaire-Rathdown Council, which includes the Dundrum area, becomes one of three new councils formed to replace Dublin County Council.
2001	Dundrum by-pass opened.
2002	In October the Dargan Luas bridge opens.
2004	On 30 June the Luas Green Line opens, using the old trackbed of the Harcourt Street line.
2005	On 3 March the Dundrum Town Centre opens.

2

BUILDINGS

CARNEGIE LIBRARY

One of the main focal points of the community in Dundrum, the Carnegie Library, was designed by an architect called Rudolph Maximilian Butler, who designed more libraries than any other Irish architect. The cost of building the new library in 1910 was a little over £1,500. It was created as one of a chain of libraries opened in Ireland and elsewhere, funded by the Scottish-American philanthropist, Andrew Carnegie.

The Carnegie Library in Dundrum was opened by the Lord Chancellor in August 1914, days after the start of the First World War. The two-storey building was, and still is, noted for the Doric columns on either side of its main entrance and the fine plasterwork on its façade. In 1973, an extensive renovation of the building was carried out by the then Dublin County Council, but the structural elements remained intact.

Today, the library has a fine array of facilities, in addition to its book collection and extensive material on local history and studies. In its earlier years, the library was also used as an entertainment centre. The upper floor had a stage, and concerts, dramas and dancing displays were put on there.

Beside the present-day library is a row of whitewashed cottages, which date from about 1850. Little changed on the exterior, they give a glimpse of what old Dundrum must have looked like in the earlier nineteenth century.

CRIMINAL LUNATIC ASYLUM

Now known as the Central Mental Hospital, this building owes its origins to the recommendations made by a parliamentary committee that had been set up in 1843 under Lord Sugden, the then Lord Chancellor. A similar facility at Broadmoor in southern England didn't open until 1863, nearly fifteen years after the opening of the institution at Windy Arbour. It took the ideological approach of treating crime and mental disorder as two sides of the same coin. The building in Windy Arbour became the first secure hospital of its kind in Europe.

Work on building the vast, forbidding block on a 14-hectare site began in 1847 and was essentially completed by 1850. The new hospital was designed by two architects from the Board of Public Works, now the Office of Public Works (OPW). One of those architects was Jacob Owen, born in Montgomeryshire in Wales in 1778. He was appointed architect and engineer of the Board of Public Works in 1832 and he remained there until his retirement in 1856.

Among the other buildings in Ireland he designed is what is now Garda headquarters in the Phoenix Park and Arbour Hill Prison. Owen was also instrumental in helping set up the Irish Civil Service Building Society in 1864, but in 1867, he left Ireland for good and settled in Hampshire. He died in England in 1870 and is buried in Dublin.

His fellow architect on the asylum scheme was Frederick Clarendon, who worked for the Board of Public Works from 1839 until he retired in 1887. His mother-in-law was a daughter of Jacob Owen.

The Central Mental Hospital site at Dundrum has long been considered unsuitable for purpose. Government policy is to sell off the site at Windy Arbour for development and relocate the hospital. Initially, the plan was to move it beside the planned new Thornton Hall Prison in north County Dublin, a plan that raised many objections and never materialised. A more recent plan is for the hospital to be transferred to a new building at Portane, also in north County Dublin.

DUNDRUM COURTHOUSE, UPPER KILMACUD ROAD

This building dates to around 1856. It was designed by two of the most distinguished Victorian architects working in Ireland, Deane and Woodward. It's sometimes said locally that the plans went to India by mistake, so that India got what should have been Dundrum's courthouse, while Dundrum got the present building, which should have been a school in India. Rebuilt after being burned down in 1923, the courthouse remained in use until the mid-1990s, but was then derelict for over a decade.

Refurbishment didn't begin until 2012 and what was once the courthouse now provides an extension of facilities for the Garda station next door, itself once described as one of the worst equipped in the country.

DUNDRUM RAILWAY STATION

This station was designed by William Dargan, built for the opening of what became the Harcourt Street line. Dargan lived nearby, at Mount Anville, and he used the station regularly to travel in and out to Dublin city centre. His involvement meant that the station was better designed and more comfortable than any of the other stations on the old line, with plenty of waiting room space and ticket offices on both sides the platform. The old station on the Taney Road side of the line survived various changes of use and still exists for the Luas line; it now houses a café. But the station building on the Dundrum Main Street side of the line has long since been demolished, as has the old footbridge.

GORT MUIRE, BALLINTEER

What is now the Gort Muire Carmelite centre and friary was designed in 1860 – its original name was Gortmore – by a renowned architect of the time, John Skipton Mulvany. He also designed the big house at Mount Anville, which became the home of William Dargan. As for Gortmore, it was such a colossal house it took ten years to complete. In 1944, Gortmore was taken over by the Irish Province of Carmelites, which had been based in Rathgar, where they were rapidly running out of space. Their Rathgar site became the original site of Mount Carmel Hospital, which closed down in 2014. Mount Carmel Hospital has now been purchased by the Health Service Executive as a step-down facility. At Gort Muire, the order started major extensions in 1946, while the new oratory was completed in 1948. For this oratory, a painting of the Scapular vision was created by renowned artist Seán Keating. A new conference centre was opened at Gort Muire in 1975 and today, the place still has a student novitiate, with Irish clerical students and indeed students from all over the world.

TANEY PARISH CENTRE

This centre was created in 1991 and is beside the existing Church of Ireland parish church at Taney. The new centre is approached by a small courtyard; light fills the courtyard from the large glazed screen and the fine stained-glass windows in the church. The interior was designed by DMOD architects to withstand heavy usage. The centre also includes a sports hall. Since its inception, the parish centre has become a very popular community venue for a wide range of local activities.

3

CHURCHES

ARMENIAN

The St Hripsime Armenian Sunday School was established in 2009, meeting in the Taney Parish Centre, where the Sunday School and other community celebrations are staged on a regular basis. Between 150 and 350 Armenians live in Ireland, so the Taney Parish Centre is a social and religious hub.

ASYLUM SERVICES

In 1867, a licence was given for Divine Service at the then almost new Criminal Lunatic Asylum in Windy Arbour. Today, Church of Ireland services are still held at the Central Mental Hospital. However, the original Church of Ireland chapel at the hospital was donated to the local Catholic parish in the late nineteenth century.

BAPTIST CHURCH

Hope Baptist Church, which is just behind the Garda station on the Upper Kilmacud Road, has been established for over ten years. Its lively congregation is led by the pastor, Dan Canavan, and among the facilities is a crèche for the children of parents attending services. People who believe that each person must experience individual salvation through a personal faith in Christ alone have met up in various forms in Dundrum from the mid-1990s onwards. In September 2004, they were organised into the Hope Baptist Church at Shamrock House on the Upper Kilmacud Road, Dundrum. By November 2011, the congregation had grown so much it moved to Taney Hall, less than 50 metres from the old place of worship.

CHRIST CHURCH, TANEY

Business and professional people started moving out of Dublin city in the eighteenth century to live in quieter rural areas and by the early nineteenth century, the move of new residents into the Dundrum area was well under way. As a result of this population shift, the new Church of Ireland church (Christ Church) at Taney was opened in 1818, becoming the principal church of the parish.

The church was extended considerably in the 1860s and 1870s, being finally consecrated in 1872. On 11 June 1872, *The Irish Times* reported on the consecration of the church the previous day by the Church of Ireland Archbishop of Dublin. The news report said that the church was 'situated in the midst of a beautiful country, prettily studded with trees and well watered: the day was on the whole very fine, a few slight showers occurring at intervals but not sufficient to mar the success of the interesting ceremony. After the proceedings were over, everyone repaired to the nearby home of Henry Roe, the wealthy Dublin whiskey distiller, who had paid for the cost of the church's renovation, the building of a new chancel and the installation of a new organ. Henry Roe lived at Mount Anville Park, where magnificent entertainment was provided for 250 people.'

This period of expansion also saw the opening of a parish school, as well as a Sunday school, and the proliferation of social clubs and other parish organisations.

Christ Church is an imposing building, both inside and out. It was designed in the Gothic Revival style and its main external feature is the square bell tower on the north side. It was designed in a cruciform shape, with fixed pew seating and a central aisle running the length of the church up to the altar. There are two timber panel-fronted balconies facing each other across the main aisle and another at the back, facing the chancel. Access to the south balcony is by the timber staircase leading from the south aisle. This staircase was dedicated as a memorial to Canon Orr, rector, 1935-1958, in October 1966, when six collecting plates were given to the church by Canon Orr's widow and family. The north balcony is reached by an elegant stone spiral staircase in the porch, under the bell tower.

The pulpit is located on the north side of the nave and beside it is the baptistry, with its carved stone font. Within the church, there are many interesting memorial plaques and windows, including, on the north wall of the chancel, a large brass memorial to the twenty people from the parish who died in the First World War. There's also a brass plaque to Everard Hamilton of Ballinteer Lodge, who died in 1925, his wife Elinor, their son Gustavus and their daughter Helen. Everard Hamilton was a solicitor, who was also a churchwarden from 1883 to 1887. He also assisted Francis Elrington Ball in writing the first history of Taney parish, published in 1895. Much more recently, in 1981, Letitia Overend from Airfield dedicated the church clock in her memory, while the chimes were presented to the church by her sister Naomi Overend.

CHURCH OF THE ASCENSION OF THE LORD, BALALLY

This parish was constituted in 1977 from Sandyford parish and it takes its name from the townland of the same name in the ancient deanery of Taney. The old Gaelic form is *Baile Amhlaoibh*, meaning the 'town of Olaf', a reference to the area's Norse heritage. The parish runs from the Slang River at Ardglas to the M50 motorway at Sandyford and takes in the housing estates on both sides of Sandyford Road, as well as estates on the Ballinteer Road, the Gort Muire conference centre and the Sandyford and Stillorgan industrial estates.

The parish has about 2,000 home and some 9,000 residents. For the first few years of the parish, St Olaf's National School was used as a Mass Centre. The strikingly modernistic church, circular, with a pink façade, was designed by renowned architect Liam McCormack, and was dedicated by the then Catholic Archbishop of Dublin, Dermot Ryan, in October 1982. Due to severe financial constraints, some parts of the church weren't finished until recent years. But when the Green Luas line was being built in the early years of the twenty-first century, the church got a windfall from the sale of some of its land to build the Luas line. This money was used to complete the church and add a new sanctuary. The church was rededicated on 1 October 2006. The first parish priest was Fr Sean Cleary, from 1977 to 1979, now deceased. He was succeeded by Fr Eddie Randles who served until 1992, when the present parish priest, Dr Dermot Lane, took over. Religious sisters connected with the parish include the Sisters of Marie Reparatrice and the Faithful Companions of Jesus.

CHURCH OF THE HOLY CROSS

For many years in the eighteenth and into the nineteenth centuries, Dundrum was part of Booterstown parish. It didn't become a parish in its own right until 1879, when Holy Cross church had been completed. About 1813, construction began on the first chapel, just off Main Street, and this work was completed before 1830. The first resident curate in Dundrum, Fr Powell, began his ministry in 1833 and shortly afterwards, the chapel was enlarged and the buildings that hid it from Main Street were taken down. An advertisement in the *Freeman's Journal*, on 27 June 1835, sought more money for the completion of the new chapel. It said that a committee had been appointed to solicit contributions to complete the enlargement of the Roman Catholic chapel of Dundrum and said that 'they most respectfully entreat the aid of their fellow citizens of every religious persuasion that they may be enabled to accomplish this desirable and indispensable work of piety'. The work was duly completed and on 14 September 1837, Dublin's Catholic Archbishop Murray arrived in the village of Dundrum to dedicate Holy Cross church.

Fr Joseph Hickey was appointed curate in Dundrum in 1865 and it was he who was faced with the task of building a new church, the present building. The current Catholic church, fronting onto Main Street, is among the most interesting ecclesiastical buildings in the area. Building started in 1877 and was completed in 1879. The church is noted for its fine sandstone façade, replicated in the adjoining presbytery. The new church cost around £5,000 to build. After all his exertions in getting the new church built, Fr Hickey lived long enough to see the fruits of his labours for a further decade, until he died in 1889.

The present church was almost doubled in length during a big extension carried out in 1953. Many of the features of the earlier church were retained, along with Sacred Heart vessels of fine late Georgian design. The 1953 extension was designed so sensitively that it retained much of the atmosphere of the 1877 design, yet created much more space as well as a hall beneath the main body of the church. Just over twenty years ago, the parish got a new parish priest, Fr Donal O'Doherty, appointed in 1993. In his twenty years with the parish, both as parish priest and pastor emeritus, he was commended by the local Catholic community for guiding the parish to its present vibrant state. In September 2013, Fr John Bracken was appointed as a co-parish priest for the team serving Dundrum, Ballinteer and Meadowbrook parishes.

In the eighteenth century, this part of Dublin was so undeveloped that one priest covered a vast area. From 1759 to 1775, the Very Revd James Nicholas was the parish priest not only of Dundrum but also of Booterstown, Donnybrook, Irishtown, Ringsend, Stillorgan and Kilmacud. All the housing development in the Dundrum area, during the later twentieth century, has meant the creation of more localised parishes.

Tony Cullen, Holy Cross Church

Tony Cullen, who died on 3 August 1964, was the clerk at Holy Cross church for fifty years. He opened and closed the doors, rang the Angelus three times a day and rang all the Mass bells. He looked after all the candles and officiated at christenings, weddings and funerals. Perhaps his hardest task was supervising the choirboys. In his earlier years, he had taken part in the War of Independence (1919-1921) and as the new state settled down, Tony Cullen became involved in innumerable public committees, as well as being a councillor on the old Dublin County Council. But Holy Cross was the centre of his life and the bachelor clerk of the church was very much an unordained priest.

Simultaneously with Tony Cullen, Kitty Delaney was the secretary of the parish, actively involved in such organisations as the Order of Malta and the Pioneer Total Abstinence Association.

CHURCH OF THE MIRACULOUS MEDAL, CLONSKEAGH

The church on Bird Avenue was built in the early 1950s in the Romanesque hybrid style, in common with Dublin church design elsewhere at that period. The church became the centre of its own parish ten years later, in 1964. The church and the new parish (hived off from Donnybrook) were designed to cater for the new housing estates that were built in the area between Dundrum and Milltown in the 1950s and 1960s. The church, which is noted for its fine mosaics, including the Stations of the Cross, has long had a problem of damp.

METHODIST CHURCH, BALLINTEER ROAD

This church was founded in January 1978 at the same time that two other Methodist churches in Dublin were closed, one at Dolphin's Barn and the other at Charleston Road, Ranelagh. The new church at Ballinteer was opened in 1979 and today, about 200 worshippers attend the two Sunday morning services.

QUAKERS

The Quaker meeting house on the Lower Churchtown Road was built in 1861 and it has been in use ever since. A local man called Charles Malone had donated the site in 1860, although he kept the mineral and hunting rights on the land as well as his rights to use the well. The meeting house cost £828 to build, but the architect is unknown. In its earlier days, it had a minister's gallery, for elders and overseers, but this was removed in 1949. The Churchtown meeting house gained members in 1930 when the meeting house at Rathmines closed down, but this trend was partially reversed after 1957, when a new meeting house was built on land at Crannagh Road, Rathfarnham, donated by Lamb Bros, the jam manufacturers. Charlie Malone's well collapsed in 1959, but the meeting house itself is still going strong. Today, the whole of Ireland has about 1,600 Quakers.

ST NAHI'S

This ancient church, with its simple boxlike structure and bell cradle, is an excellent reminder of what both Catholic and Protestant churches looked like in the seventeenth and eighteenth centuries. Also called St Nahi's, the present church was built in the early eighteenth century (its

earliest grave is dated 1734) and one of its interesting artefacts is the font in which the future Duke of Wellington was baptised in 1769. It came from an old church in Camden Row in the centre of Dublin.

The original St Nahi's was built around AD 600, and a monastery was located beside it, but needless to remark, any trace of those first buildings on this site has long since disappeared.

The last major renovation of the church was carried out in 1910 by Revd Monk Gibbon, who was vicar of both this church and the one at Taney for twenty-four years, until he died on 26 March 1935. His son, also Monk Gibbon (1896-1987) was often called the Grand Old Man of Irish Letters.

This 1910 renovation was carried out after a period when the church had also been used as the local boys' national school. Regular Church of Ireland services are still held at St Nahi's. After the disestablishment of the Church of Ireland in 1869, it became possible for people of all denominations in the area to be buried at St Nahi's, which has about 2,000 graves in its hillside graveyard beside the Dargan Luas bridge. Altogether, about 10,000 people have been buried here since the eighteenth century, although Christians have been buried on the site of St Nahi's for at least 1,000 years. There is a communal grave for people who were once inmates of the old lunatic asylum at Windy Arbour, renamed the Central Mental Hospital in 1961.

Among those buried at St Nahi's are many Republicans, including Lorcain McSwuibhne, a member of the old IRA, who was killed in County Kildare in 1922 and whose funeral at St Nahi's was attended by Eamon de Valera. Christopher Reynolds, an IRA volunteer killed by British soldiers in 1921, is also buried there. Many Royal Irish Constabulary officers and Freemasons are also buried at St Nahi's, which is the last resting place of one local casualty from the Second World War, Sergeant William Kavanagh, who was killed in action in 1944. He was the son of William and Mary Kavanagh from Dundrum.

Buried there too are three members of the Yeats family: Elizabeth and Susan, daughters of John Butler Yeats, brother of W.B. Yeats, and Grainne Yeats, daughter of W.B. Yeats.

Some embroidered work done at Dun Emer in its early days in Dundrum can also be seen in the church.

In July 2008, politician and government minister Seamus Brennan was buried there.

St Nahi's feast day is 9 August and the saint was the first person to set up a religious settlement in the Dundrum area. He is credited with having started a centre for monastic life in the seventh century, on the site of the old St Nahi's church in Dundrum. Indeed one explanation of the name 'Taney' is that it comes from '*Teach Naithi*', or 'Nahi's house'.

Religious worship was known to have taken place on the site well before the Anglo-Norman conquest in the late twelfth century. By the middle of that century it had become a rural see, while by the thirteenth century it embraced parishes as far away as Coolock, Cloghran and Chapelizod. The present St Nahi's church dates back to the middle of the eighteenth century and was consecrated on 8 June 1760. The church is noted for its stained-glass windows, most of which were created by artists belonging to the An Túr Gloine (The Tower of Glass) group of artists active in the first half of the twentieth century. Three artists in particular produced outstanding

stained-glass windows for St Nahi's – Alfred Ernest Child, Catherine O'Brien and Ethel Rhind. Later, in 1933, Evie Hone created several stained-glass windows for the church. She had been born at Roebuck Grove in 1894 and several of her ancestors had lived in Dundrum during the eighteenth century. She was a direct descendant of the great eighteenth-century painter, Nathaniel Hone.

TANEY PARISH

In 1152, a report was made of the rural see of Taney. Following on from that, although the exact date is unknown, was a taxation list sent from Rome to the diocese of Dublin. The evidence is clear; religious worship was very well established in the Dundrum area long before the Anglo-Norman invasion.

After the invasion, Henry II granted Leinster to Richard de Clare (Strongbow), but Tacheny or Taney was one of the two areas held back. It was allocated to Hugh de Clahull, who later gave his lands in the Dublin area to the Archbishop of Dublin. In the Papal Bull of 1179, there is a reference to 'the middle place of Tighney', with a church extant there and three subsidiary chapels, at Donnybrook, Kilgobbin and Rathfarnham.

By the early thirteenth century, the rural deanery of Taney was well established. Archbishop Luke (1228-1255) established that Taney was a prebend of St Patrick's Cathedral in Dublin and until 1851, the archdeacons of Dublin held the prebendary and the post of rector of Taney. From then until the mid-nineteenth century, the parish in Taney was mainly overseen by curates-in-charge.

At some point in the sixteenth century, from the separation between King Henry VIII and Rome and Queen Elizabeth I, the parish of Taney became part of the State church. The Roman Catholic heritage of the district eventually became part of a Union parish, overseen from Booterstown. But in the middle of the sixteenth century, Taney parish was still going strong. In 1546, Taney parish was recorded as having annual rentals worth £19, enough to pay the salary of the resident curate. The site of the present-day church at St Nahi's was long the original parish church.

But by 1630, the church at St Nahi's was reported to have been in poor condition, with only two householders attending. Most of the local population still adhered to the teachings of the Catholic Church. The church at St Nahi's was rebuilt in 1760 and the new building was consecrated on 8 June that year. But it wasn't to last long. A mere fifty years later, discussions were well underway about providing a brand new church on the present location at Taney. The decision to build was made in 1814 and the initial consecration took place on 21 June 1818, although it wasn't fully consecrated until 1872.

Taney's Resident Organist

Maureen Maguire was a long-time resident in Taney. She worked in the Robert Roberts Tea and Coffee Company and was long the organist at St Mary's church in Sandyford. She died in March 2014, in her ninety-sixth year.

4

CRIME AND MAYHEM

DROWNING IN THE RIVER DODDER

On 10 October 1782, during heavy rain, a Mr Clarke, steward of the House of Industry in Dundrum, was returning home to Milltown. At about nine o'clock that night, on horseback, he crossed the River Dodder. The flood was so violent that he was thrown off his horse and drowned. His daughter and only child had been drowned in the same river twelve months previously.

DUNDRUM'S BEADLE

In the late eighteenth century, the churchwardens at the Church of Ireland in Taney employed a beadle, who was responsible for keeping law and order in the district. The churchwardens also provided the finance to erect a set of stocks in Dundrum, but it's not known where they stood or how often they were used.

DUNDRUM BARRACKS ATTACKED

In 1867, the police barracks in Dundrum was attacked by a group of Fenian supporters, who also attacked neighbouring barracks in Milltown, Stepaside and Glencullen. But the Fenians were unable to either capture or damage any of the barracks. The man who led the raids was called Patrick Lennon who was described as a kindly faced, priestly looking man who neither smoked nor drank. After the unsuccessful raids, he escaped to County Wicklow and soon afterwards managed to flee to England.

IRA VOLUNTEER PATRICK DOYLE KILLED IN 1916

On 27 April 1916, an IRA volunteer from Milltown was killed during the Battle of Mount Street Bridge. His name was Patrick Doyle, a Church of Ireland man who had a respectable job as a manager with the Milltown Laundry. But he was devoted to the nationalist cause and was a keen advocate of the Irish language. He left behind his wife and children to take part in the 1916 Easter Rising and when IRA units ambushed British troops at Mount Street bridge, he was in one of those units. The troops had been landed at Kingstown (now Dún Laoghaire), and had marched in from there. A bloody battle followed at Mount Street bridge, with heavy casualties on both sides.

Patrick Doyle was one of the IRA men inside Clanwilliam House, close to the bridge, and he and his comrades fired devastatingly on the soldiers below. Eventually, the British commanders at the scene decided to storm Clanwilliam House which caught fire and was completely destroyed. Doyle was one of three IRA men who lost their lives in the fire. Doyle was buried at St Nahi's in Dundrum, although some stories suggest that the fire in Clanwilliam House was so intense that there was nothing left of the three IRA men to bury.

Doyle's son, also Patrick, was killed taking part in an IRA ambush at Crooksling, County Dublin, on 7 July 1922.

CROKE PARK SPECTATOR MURDERED IN 1920

James Burke was one of the innocent spectators at Croke Park on Bloody Sunday, 21 November 1920, who was murdered by British soldiers. A native of the Dundrum area, he was buried at St Nahi's.

FIRST FEMALE JPS

The first female Justices of the Peace were appointed following the passing of the Sex Disqualification (Removal) Act, 1919. The first case before a female magistrate in Ireland took place soon afterwards, at the petty sessions in Dundrum, when Lady Redmond took her seat with the other JPs, on Monday, 16 February 1920. She was one of four female JPs appointed at the time.

FUTURE MINISTER FOR JUSTICE SLEPT IN DUNDRUM ON THE RUN

During the War of Independence, Kevin O'Higgins, who later became the first Minister for Justice in the new Irish Free State, and who was assassinated at Booterstown in 1927, often slept in the Dundrum area whilst on the run. He had a string attached to his feet so that he could be woken at a moment's notice if he had to make a run for it in the face of an impending raid. IRA volunteers frequently hid in the long grass on the railway embankments close to the railway station, to observe what was going on.

CHRISTOPHER REYNOLDS

On 1 April 1921, an IRA volunteer called Christopher Reynolds, who by day was a clerk with the New Ireland Assurance company, was killed by British soldiers close to Portobello bridge in Rathmines after he had escaped from their custody when their tender broke down. Previously, Reynolds had been arrested at his home in Rathfarnham. He was buried at St Nahi's.

CLASSON'S BRIDGE, MILLTOWN, BLOWN UP BY THE IRA

Classon's bridge at Milltown, which dated from the eighteenth century, was blown up by a local IRA unit in 1921, after several previous and unsuccessful attempts. The bridge wasn't reinstated for seven years, which meant that anyone who wanted to approach the Milltown golf club, or go to the few houses that then existed on what was then the cul de sac of Lower Churchtown Road, had to cross the River Dodder on a rickety makeshift bridge made from planks. To this day, plaques commemorating the building of the new bridge can be seen on its sides.

BLACK AND TANS IN DUNDRUM

Following the 1916 Easter Rising, the War of Independence began in 1919 and continued until a truce was agreed in July 1921. Black and Tan auxiliary soldiers, many of them men released from prisons in Britain, were shipped to Ireland to try and restore order. Instead, they terrorised local communities. Main Street in Dundrum was frequently sealed off by Black and Tan roadblocks, even though the volume of traffic was a fraction of what it is today. In those days, Main Street had more horses than cars.

When the truce was declared in July 1921, a celebratory bonfire was lit at the crossroads in Dundrum. The town was lucky; it wasn't burned down by the Black and Tans, unlike other towns such as Balbriggan.

DUNDRUM POLICE BARRACKS ATTACKED 1923

Dundrum's police barracks, where the present-day Garda station is situated, on the Upper Kilmacud Road, was attacked and destroyed during the 1922-23 Civil War. Irregulars stormed the building and set fire to it on Wednesday, 26 January 1923, completely destroying the building. However, other sources say that the raid on the police barracks didn't happen until Friday morning, 2 February 1923.

Subsequently, questions were asked in the Dáil about how a police station so close to the city could be attacked and destroyed in this manner. The police station was rebuilt and this rebuild lasted until 1970, when the present Garda station replaced it. In the same 1923 raid, the adjoining courthouse was also burned down and subsequently rebuilt.

CENTRAL MENTAL ASYLUM ATTACK

In 1923, a man called Patrick Gaffney, who was an attendant at the asylum in Windy Arbour, was paid compensation for injuries suffered when he was attacked while on duty at the hospital. Subsequently, between 1940 and 1942, in the early years of the Second World War, much consideration was given to the idea of transferring patients from the asylum to the prison at Portlaoise, although nothing came of the proposal.

IRA MAN GEORGE GILMORE HELPS COMRADE TO ESCAPE

In 1926, George Gilmore, a well-known republican, managed to engineer an amazing escape at Windy Arbour. He managed to spring an unnamed IRA man from the asylum at Windy Arbour and make good his escape. During the last few years of the 1920s, Gilmore and his brother Harry dominated the IRA in south Dublin, including the Dundrum area. George Gilmore lived to a grand old age, being 87 when he died in 1985.

BALLINTEER MAN IN IRA RAID

Just as the Second World War started, the IRA staged a daring raid on the magazine fort in the Phoenix Park, escaping with a considerable amount of armaments and ammunition. One of those arrested in connection with this raid was a man called William Cleary, who lived in Ballinteer. He was arrested at the end of December 1939.

DUNDRUM'S THIRD REICH SUPPORTERS

In the early stages of the Second World War, known in Ireland as the 'Emergency', Dundrum had a number of active supporters of the Third Reich in Germany. One of them was Captain Liam Walsh of Highfield Park, Dundrum, who held a meeting of the Irish Friends of Germany at his home on 14 April 1940. He was subsequently arrested and interned, from April until October 1940.

Another person from the general area who was interned for having similar political views, was George Plunkett from Owenstown House on Foster Avenue. He was kept inside from May 1940 to June 1944. Meanwhile, a near neighbour of Captain Walsh had been arrested in the summer of 1940 for possessing ammunition. He was John Turley, who also lived in Highfield Park.

SKULL DISCOVERY AT DUNDRUM CASTLE

The ruins of Dundrum Castle were bought in 1984 by David Johnston, an authority on old castles who has published several books on the subject. The castle is now a National Monument and is still owed by Johnston. A skull, but no body, was found when an old rose bed near the sixteenth-century part of the castle was being cleared. Forensic examination showed that it belonged to a man aged between 25 and 30. He had evidently met a violent death, as his skull had been broken into four separate pieces. At the time of the discovery, it was thought the remains dated back to medieval times, but they turned out to be much more recent. The identity of the victim was never discovered and neither did it prove possible to discover when the murder had taken place.

GARDA STATION MAKEOVER COMPLETED

In 2011, it was announced that Dundrum Garda station, on the Upper Kilmacud Road, was to be refurbished and extended. Improvements to the Dundrum station had long been a priority for the Garda Representative Association, which in its 1993 list of over 100 under-equipped Garda stations, had rated Dundrum as the second worst. This station dated back to 1970, when the two-storey, flat-roofed building, devoid of any redeeming architectural characteristics, replaced the earlier barracks, which had been built to replace the police barracks burned down in 1923.

5

HOUSES AND MANSIONS

AIRFIELD

Airfield, situated close to Ballaly, is one of Dublin's great heritage attractions. It all began in 1894 when Trevor Overend, a wealthy Dublin solicitor, bought an eighteenth-century farmhouse, which he had rebuilt as a fine mansion. He and his wife maintained the household there until their deaths, then their two daughters, Letitia and Naomi, took over. They lived the rest of their lives here, running both the big house and the surrounding 15-hectare farm, noted for its Jersey cows. When the Overends arrived at Airfield, the surrounding land only amounted to just over 3 hectares, so Trevor Overend oversaw a substantial expansion of the family's land holdings.

During the First World War, wounded soldiers often came to stay at the house, considered an ideal place to recuperate. In 1920, as can be seen from correspondence on view in the house, Letitia was offered an OBE for all her charity work, but she politely declined. She was very involved in the St John's Ambulance Brigade and its Overend Hall in Upper Leeson Street, Dublin, is named after her.

From the 1920s onwards, the sisters bought more land to expand the farm. They maintained the house, in between other activities, such as travelling the world. At the house, they had a cook called Mary Barry, who was stone deaf, so all the instructions to her had to be written down.

Apart from the house in Dundrum, the sisters also had a holiday home, first at Port Salon in north County Donegal and then at Brittas Bay in County Wicklow.

The sisters maintained three cars, a 1927 Rolls Royce, an Austin 10 Tickford and a Peugeot Quadrilette. The Quadrilette had been bought in 1923 for £230, while the Rolls Royce was used by Letitia for over sixty years, as shown in the logbooks.

Letitia was in the habit of going to Dundrum, then little more than a sleepy country village, and parking the car where she felt like it, along Main Street, sometimes far out from the kerb! Yet in those days, long before parking wardens were thought of, nobody bothered with such motoring indiscretions. In 1974, three years before Letitia's death, the Overend family made the far-sighted decision to turn the house and the estate into a trust, so that after the death of the two sisters, everything would be maintained. It wasn't the first time by any means that the Overends had made charitable decisions that benefitted the locality. In 1967, they gave one of their fields to Taney Church of Ireland parish to build a new primary school.

Naomi died in 1993 and since then, under the trust, chaired by John Edmondson, the house itself has been well restored. In the main ground floor living rooms, easy to use interactive technology enables visitors of all ages to explore the history of the house and estate, while such artefacts as old newspapers and old suitcases and lots of photographs, add to the historical narrative. The official opening of the newly-restored house and estate, fully refurbished, took place in April 2014, when the Minister for Agriculture, Food, the Marine and Defence Simon Coveney, did the honours.

Besides the house, the garage has the sisters' three cars, in a perfect state of preservation, with interactive technology revealing all the details. The farm is back in action again and visitors can see demonstrations of butter-, cream- and cheese-making. The walled garden, the tea garden and the greenhouse garden have all been restored, while the new kitchen garden has its own maze, vineyard and herb collection. Complementing all the delights of the estate is the modern Overend café, where vegetables, herbs, eggs, fruit and dairy produce from the farm are used in the cooking. The only blot on the horizon at Airfield is the succession of high-rise apartment blocks in Balally, to the immediate south of the estate, which spoil the view of the Dublin mountains.

BALALLY'S FIRST HOUSE

Balally, just before the village of Sandyford, is an ancient townland, whose previous name was Ballawley. Before that, it was known as Bellewly. The first recorded house here was built in 1280, when John de Walhope was given permission to cut down seven oak trees in the royal forest at Glencree and use them to build a house for himself on the townland. Nearly four centuries later, in 1654, when the townland was still entirely rural, a thatched castle was described here, with the adjoining walls of an old chapel. The property was owned by the Walshe family, who two years later, in 1656, sold the property to Christian Borr for £700. There is no record of this castle surviving and even its exact location is now unknown.

BALALLY TERRACE, BALALLY

This terrace of council houses was built around 1900 and is one of the earliest examples of council housing in the whole Dundrum area. The houses were two-storey dwellings, as opposed to the single-storey council houses built slightly later, in the early years of the twentieth century, at Ballyogan Road, Kilgobbin and Murphystown Road. The name of Balally is now applied to a whole area of privately developed estates created in the 1960s and 1970s.

CASINO, WINDY ARBOUR

This manor house on Bird Avenue was once occupied by the family of Robert Emmet, who was executed in 1803. The house is now known as Emmet House and is occupied by the Secretariat of the Secondary Schools of Ireland. This large, square house once had a viewing platform on the roof, an unusual feature. The interior is plainly decorated, but includes an attractive semi-circular hall and a very large drawing room. The spacious grounds and gardens still exist. In Robert Emmet's time, his bedroom in the house had a secret trapdoor leading to a passageway that went beneath the lawns to the summerhouse. He was a much wanted man at the time and this escape route was essential for his safety.

CLONARD

This fine Victorian mansion still survives today, off the road from Dundrum to Sandyford. It was once home to Henry Thompson of Thompson and D'Olier, noted wine merchants in Victorian Dublin. Today, it is part of the Irish Management Institute.

COMMERCIALLY BUILT ESTATES

Since the early 1950s, many commercially developed estates have changed the face of the Dundrum area. The 1950s saw the development of St Luke's Crescent, Milltown (1952), Goatstown Road (1953), Ballinteer Road (1954), Wyckham Road (1954) and Drummartin estate, Goatstown (1958).

In the 1960s, new estates included Farranboley Park in Milltown (1966).

The 1970s saw a spate of estate building, including Churchtown House (1972), Ballinteer Close (1973), Ludford Drive (1973), Lissadell estate, Broadford Road, Ballinteer (1973), Chestnut Grove, Ballinteer (1974), Taney Rise (1974) and Lynwood, Ballinteer (1977).

During the 1980s, this rush of new estate construction continued unabated. The Llewellyn estate in Ballinteer was built in 1980 as was Glasson Court, Beech Lawn (1982), Taney Manor (1985), Harlech Downs, Roebuck (1988) and developments at Shields institute (1989).

In the 1990s, developments included those at Simpson's Hospital (1994) and Dundrum Castle House (1998). In more recent times, before the 2008 economic crash, new estates included Milltown Bridge estate, Milltown (2001) and Frankfort Court, Dundrum (2002).

COUNCIL ESTATES

Numerous council estates have also been developed in the Dundrum area since 1950. They include, in order of their construction, Mulvey Park (1950), Patrick Doyle Road (1952), Rosemount Estate (1970), Rosemount Court (1974), Glasson Court (1981), McGrane Court (1988), St Joseph's Grove (1993), Rosemount Way (1994), Rosemount Glade (1998) and Magenta Terrace (2003).

DROMMARTIN CASTLE

Drommartin Castle was built in the late eighteenth century, after Lord Fitzwilliam had given permission to Patrick D'Arcy to set up a brickworks at Drummartin. The castle was an attractive Georgian house, but it was demolished in 1984. Both it and Campfield, designed in the Gothic style, were situated between the Kilmacud and Taney roads. Campfield was demolished in 1985. All the grounds of Campfield were subsequently built over.

DUNDRUM CASTLE AND HOUSE

Dundrum Castle still survives as a medieval ruin. It was built by Richard Fitzwilliam in 1590 on the site of an earlier thirteenth-century castle. It was granted to William Fitzwilliam in 1365 and it was the seat of the Fitzwilliam family for a time, but they eventually moved to Baggotrath, close to present-day Upper Baggot Street. Dundrum Castle was rebuilt by Sir Richard Fitzwilliam in the 1590s. This created a substantial castle with walls around 15 metres high. The last Fitzwilliam to reside at Dundrum Castle was William Fitzwilliam, the third Viscount Fitzwilliam, who had left by 1653, although the Fitzwilliam family continued to own the castle and lands for over another century.

During the 1641 rebellion, the castle fell into disrepair, but twelve years later, it was restored and then occupied by Lt Col. Dobson, who was with Cromwell's army. At this time, the castle grounds were greatly improved. A flower garden was laid out, with trim box

borders and neatly cut yew trees, with an adjacent pleasure ground and kitchen garden. All of these features were surrounded by a grove of ash trees, presenting a picturesque sight. The grounds of the castle sloped down to the banks of the River Slang, so the whole scene must have looked idyllic. *The History of Dublin* (1902) by Francis Elrington Ball described the castle as being in good condition, with a slate roof, three hearths and an adjacent barn.

Dobson died in 1700. His son Eliphal, an alderman on Dublin Corporation and also the wealthiest bookseller and publisher in Dublin, continued to live in the castle. Besides his wealth and his position in society, he was also remarkable for his wooden leg, which replaced a leg he had lost in an accident. His wooden leg was said to have creaked horribly. Alderman Dobson died in 1720 and by 1780 the castle had been taken over by a wealthy silk weaver called Thomas Reynolds, but it was deteriorating. Reynolds was more interested in cutting down the ash trees to make money from the timber than with maintaining the castle.

After 1790, the castle started to fall into serious disrepair although a drawing from 1802 showed it was still in reasonable external condition. By the early nineteenth century, it had fallen into ruin and remains that way today.

The ruin of the castle is now on the western side of the Dundrum bypass, which follows the course of the river. Just over ten years ago, when the Dundrum Town Centre was being built, there was talk of

the old castle being turned into a heritage centre, but nothing ever came of the idea. The eighteenth-century Dundrum Castle House was a substantial residential property, although by the mid-twentieth century it had been converted to commercial use. Ilford Ireland, makers and suppliers of photographic equipment, was based here for a number of years. Finally, Dundrum Castle House was demolished in 1996 and apartments were then built on the site; unsurprisingly, they are known as Dundrum Castle House apartments. In its heyday it was typical of a mansion of that period, complete with single-storey symmetrical wings.

ENDERLEY, SWEETMOUNT AVENUE

This seventeenth-century house at the top of Sweetmount Avenue in Dundrum is typical of the earlier big houses that existed in the area, but few of them have survived to the present. This sprawling house, covers 271 square metres and is set on 0.5 hectares of land. On those lands are an orchard, stables and outbuildings, as well as a vast, old-fashioned garden, all reminiscent of old Dundrum. The garden was spectacular in its heyday, so much so that the Plant Society used to do regular conducted tours there. In the early 1960s, the owner, a keen horsewoman, used to ride out from her stables and trot across largely open country as far as Ticknock. Enderley is actually a semi-detached house, although it isn't immediately obvious, as a high wall divides it from the neighbouring house.

FARRANBOLEY COTTAGES, WINDY ARBOUR

Farranboley Cottages, along with Farranboley Park, recall the original name at the heart of the district, Farranboley, which comes from the Irish phrase, '*Fearann Buaile*', or 'territory of the milking place'. Farranboley became one of the twenty parishes making up the parish of Taney. In the 1930s, Dublin County Council built a large number of houses here to replace the many old cottages and cabins in the district. But there are still many old cottages and terraced houses in Windy Arbour, such as Woodbine Terrace and Rosemount Terrace, which backs onto the River Slang. The long row of houses, about sixteen in all, that form Millmount Terrace, were built by the laundry in Milltown for some of its employees.

FRANKFORT CASTLE

This was built in 1858-9 on the site of what had been Frankfort Lodge. It has simple castellations on its front elevation, but no historical significance. Frankfort Villa was built about ten years later on a greenfield site and is now Frankfort House in Frankfort Park.

HOMESTEAD

Now the headquarters of the Pallotine Fathers, this big house, beside the old road from Dundrum to Balally, dates back to around 1825. In the eighteenth century a big house called Runnymede stood on the site, occupying 15 hectares of land. The new house, Homestead, was occupied by a number of well-to-do residents. Joseph Collen of the noted family of builders, lived there from 1910 until his death in 1941. When St Nahi's church in Dundrum was re-roofed and extensively renovated in 1910, it was the Collen firm that did the job. The Collen family also maintained extensive gardens at Homestead and won frequent prizes at the Royal Dublin Society show for their flowers.

Homestead was sold in 1965 to a company called Home Rentals, controlled by property developer James Gallagher, who was also a Fianna Fáil TD. Eventually, Gallagher and his wife Mary, who had been living in Homestead, did a deal with the Pallotines, under which they swopped the Pallotine's student residence in Stillorgan for Homestead.

The deal was done in 1978, seven years after the Pallotines had decided to move their provincial house from London to Dublin. Since 1979, up to the present, over seventy students have come to Homestead to study for the priesthood. In 1983, the surviving Pallotine trustees conveyed Homestead to the St Vincent Palotti Trust (Ireland).

The basic fabric of the old house remains largely unaltered, with many of its original features still in place. From the west side of the house, there are views out on to the rose garden and the conservatory, while the north side faces out towards the redbrick studentate, Palotti House, which has been in use since it was built in 1979. Palotti House was built in the kitchen garden and orchard. In the grounds are the garage and coach house with the old stables, which may have been used as a dairy when the Homestead estate extended to its full 3.65 hectares.

MILL HOUSE

This ancient house on the former main road just south of Dundrum village dates back over 300 years and was certainly in a good state of repair in the mid-eighteenth century. It was originally the home of the miller from the adjacent mill that stood on the site before the laundry was opened in 1864. Right up to the time the Dundrum Town Centre was built, the house was still a private dwelling, occupied by the Dillon Digby family, which had a close connection with the old Pye Radio factory at the back of the house.

Since the development of the adjacent Dundrum Town Centre, it has been turned into a fine restaurant, run by Roly Saul.

The street façade of the house, which dates back to at least 1730, is covered by a preservation order, so it cannot be altered, but at the back of the restaurant, mainly glass-covered extensions have been put in place. A glass two-storey structure overlooks the Mill Pond in the Dundrum Town Centre. Gerry Cahill Architects were responsible for the renovation of the house and the new extension, creating a bar area, private dining rooms, a meeting room and an outdoor restaurant. The aim, says Roly Saul, was to design a restaurant with state-of-the-art technology while at the same time, retaining the charm of the old house. Diners can now enjoy sumptuous meals on the first floor of the new conservatory, looking out on the Mill Pond.

One celebrated photo from Dundrum, probably taken in the early 1930s, as Fianna Fáil came to power for the first time, shows Eamon de Valera, founder of the party and later Taoiseach and then President, striding past the Mill House, with a veritable army of admirers in tow. Tom Kitt, who comes from Galway, like another Fianna Fáil TD for Dublin South, the late Seamus Brennan, was a TD for the constituency from 1987 until 2011. His constituency office was in Pembroke House, at Glenville Terrace on Main Street in Dundrum, and pride of place there was given to a copy of this photograph of the day de Valera came to Dundrum.

MOREEN, SANDYFORD

This late eighteenth-century house, with its beautiful grove of beech trees, was purchased to become the currency production centre of the Central Bank of Ireland. The house was built by William McKay, a solicitor and a captain in the Dragoon Guards. The family was devoted to hunting and riding and in the 1850s, steeple races were staged there. The house was demolished to make way for the currency centre but the foundations of a ninth-century church are still in place. When the nearby M50 was being built, the area around the church was excavated for archaeological remains. There are also indications that the Pale Ditch, a prehistoric thoroughfare, passed close by. A bank of soil, planted with trees, and stretching for about 240 metres on the estate, is thought to be a remnant of the Pale Ditch.

MOUNT ANVILLE

Once the home of William Dargan (1799-1867), the railway pioneer, who built the railway that passed through Dundrum from Dublin on the way to Bray. The house was designed in the Italianate style, probably between 1790 and 1801. Details of the house's construction are sketchy. It had several owners before Dargan, including the Hon. Charles Burton, a well-respected judge. Another previous owner was Henry Roe, a wealthy Dublin distiller. At Mount Anville, Roe employed a chef, Michael Jammet, whom he had brought from the south of Ireland. Jammet subsequently was in charge of catering at the Viceregal Lodge in the Phoenix Park (now Áras an Uachtaráin, the residence of the President) and in Dublin Castle and then opened his famous restaurant in Dublin city centre in 1901.

Once William Dargan and his wife Jane moved into Mount Anville, they set about improving the Italianate-style villa. Dargan also developed the farm beside the house and in his time, chickens, geese and sheep were reared there. Dargan was also responsible for the building of the greenhouses, which were used for growing vines. The head gardener and steward with Dargan was James Byrne, who continued in that position after Mount Anville became a school run by the Society of the Sacred Heart, in 1866.

Dargan received Queen Victoria at the house during her visit to Ireland in 1853. She pressed him to accept a baronetcy, but he declined the honour. Later, Dargan was riding his horse one day on the Stillorgan road when a woman shook a bedsheet out of a house window. This frightened Dargan's horse and he was thrown from it. He never recovered from his injuries, and as his health declined, he sold Mount Anville.

OVEREND HOUSE

This fine house was one of the first big modern dwellings built in Dundrum and it was done on a lavish scale in 1937, designed by the architectural practice of W.M. Mitchell & Sons, Dublin, and built by Cramptons, the Dublin-based builders. This substantial modern home was built for G.A. Overend – related to the Overends at Airfield – a solicitor and a director of Dublin Cinemas. Most of this house on the Kilmacud Road was two storey, but a wing of the house rises to three stories.

PEMBROKE COTTAGES

These distinctive cottages were named after the Pembroke estate, on whose land they were built. Close on twenty were built along Main Street in Dundrum, with a further terrace at the back of that row. The lanes connecting the two rows of houses had rows of smaller scale, three-bay single-storey houses. Another set of Pembroke cottages was built in Dundrum, on the Ballinteer Road, but on a much smaller scale, being three pairs of semi-detached houses. Six more were built just beyond the crossroads and these were eventually bought for £600 by the Manor Mill Laundry to house some of its managers. Besides Dundrum, the same style of cottage was built in other southside areas, such as Booterstown, Donnybrook and Ringsend. These cottages were

all built as housing for workers and labourers on the Pembroke estate. The ones in Dundrum were built by a local man, John Richardson, whose family home and business was nearby, on Main Street. The bricks used in their construction came from the local brickworks. The cottages were built about 140 years ago, by John Richardson, who lived nearby on Main Street and who ran his building business from his house. As for the rents, they were quite expensive for the time, just under three shillings a week.

Although the cottages have a very distinctive style, it's unclear who the architect was, although James Owen, an architect with the Board of Public Works, had a supervisory role in their construction.

PEMBROKE LODGE, MAIN STREET

This house was built on Main Street in Dundrum in the mid-nineteenth century by William Richardson, as a family home. It was reputed to have been the first slated building in the village. Richardson also ran his building firm from the house and he was reputed to have built all the redbrick buildings that exist to this day in Dundrum.

Four generations of the Richardson family lived here, over a 100-year time span. However, one mystery remains: the exact date when the house was built. Ronan Lee from Dundrum, who has a particular interest in the old building and the Richardson family, says that he has never been able to find any reference to the exact date of the house.

When the last of the Richardson family to live in the house died in 1980, the house was sold to the then new Dundrum Credit Union, which established its first proper office there. It eventually became the site of the modern premises of the organisation.

ROEBUCK PARK

This fine Victorian house was to the west of the Goatstown Road, and was noted for its granite portico and elegant interior. It was demolished in 1996.

ROSEMOUNT

The old railway bridge at Dundrum separated Dundrum from the district of Rosemount, on the road to Windy Arbour. Close on a century ago, living conditions in houses at Rosemount were some of the worst in the whole district, with no indoor sanitation. One collection of cottages had a single outdoor lavatory for fifty cottages at Rosemount. Residents usually had to get their water from kerbside fountains, one of which was almost beside the present Joe Daly's cycle shop. Rosemount has a number of terraces at right-angles to the main road, including Alexandra Terrace and Victoria Terrace. Magenta Lane has long since been demolished and its former entrance is now Rosemount Park.

RUNNIMEDE OR DUN EMER

This eighteenth-century house stood on the main road to Sandyford and when the Dun Emer Guild was established there in 1903, the name of the house was changed to Dun Emer, which continues in use.

WINDY ARBOUR HOUSE

This house was built in 1850 by a newspaper publisher called W. Stanley Purdon. He and his brother ran the *Farmers' Gazette* newspaper, whose offices were at Bachelor's Walk in the city centre. When the house was built for himself in what was then a largely rural area, he called it Windy Arbour House. However, the development of residential roads in Windy Arbour didn't begin in earnest until the 1920s and 1930s.

WYCKHAM

This fine late Georgian house was built around 1800 and it was a family home until 1825, when it was sold to Simpson's Hospital, which then moved from Parnell Street in Dublin city centre to Dundrum. The hospital had been founded in Dublin in 1791 for 'reduced gentlemen, suffering from failing eyesight, gout or both'. Its benefactor was George Simpson, who had begun life as a penniless orphan and who made his fortune in Dublin retailing. He founded the hospital to look after men suffering from similar ailments to himself. The hospital was in Parnell Street, in the city centre, before moving out to Dundrum. The Parnell Street building became a confectionery factory for Williams & Woods in 1876 and the building was demolished in 1978.

The three-storey mansion at Ballinteer Road in Dundrum still forms the centrepiece of the hospital, complete with its more modern additions. The house is distinguished by an extensive portico, topped by a balustrade, at its front entrance.

In a recent €4 million scheme, the main house was refurbished and the conservatory at the back was rebuilt, while a new two-storey extension was built at one side of the house. The hospital, which is now described as a nursing home, changed its charter so that it can now look after both men and women, from all walks of life and of all denominations.

WYCKHAM POINT

In February 2014 it was announced that a property company, Hibernian REIT, had acquired a portfolio of residential properties from the Ulster Bank for €67 million. Among those properties was a long-running eyesore in Dundrum, consisting of 213 partly completed apartments at Wyckham Point, one of the casualties of the collapse of the property market during the recession. The purchasers said they were going to invest €20 million in completing the apartments, which they then intended to rent out. Wyckham Point was just one of a number of ghost estates in the area, left unfinished when the 'Celtic Tiger' economic boom collapsed in 2007 and 2008. By 2010, it was estimated that south Dublin, including Dundrum and Sandyford, had a total of forty-nine ghost estates, with a total of nearly 9,500 units. At that stage, 760 of them were still under construction, while a further 1,286 were completed, but vacant.

6

NATURAL HISTORY

AIRFIELD

This heritage house and farm has lots of natural history, including a wonderful garden that has been redesigned and refurbished by noted landscape designer Arabella Lennox-Boyd and there's a refurbished walled garden and a tea garden, as well as the brand new food garden, where seasonal food is grown. The vineyard is an unusual addition to the kitchen garden, as is the display of native Irish apple trees. The kitchen is where seasonal food-based education and events take place, while Airfield also has some trial planting beds for experimenting with different combinations of crops and herbs. Visitors can also see the workings of the farm, from the twice-daily milking of the Jersey herd to egg collecting, mucking out and feeding.

The new farmyard contains livestock housing and stables. Visitors have easy access to the animals, the milking parlour and the dairy kitchen. Throughout the year, events like lambing, calving and sheep shearing can be observed. The working farm at Airfield not only has Jersey cows and sheep, but pigs, chickens and donkeys. The farm has fifty laying hens, including Rhode Island Red Hybrids and fancy fowl such as Legbars and Arucanas. Food from the gardens and the farm is used in the stylishly modern adjoining Overend café.

When the Overend sisters, Letitia and Naomi, owned the estate, they raised many cattle on the farm and during the Second World War emergency, extensive crops were grown. Not surprisingly, one of the highlights of the year for the sisters was the former Spring Show at the RDS.

In the woodland area, 2,000 native Irish trees have been planted, while the grounds of Airfield – apart from the farm and the gardens – have a pet cemetery.

BALLAWLEY PARK

Just off Sandyford Road, this quiet, well-maintained park includes an outdoor gym.

MARLAY PARK

On the edge of Ballinteer, Marlay Park, extending for 121 hectares, is one of the largest parks in south Dublin. It has extensive footpaths as well as cycle paths and many sporting facilities, including five GAA pitches, six soccer pitches and a nine-hole golf course. It also has two playgrounds for children and in summer, outdoor concerts are staged here. The eighteenth-century Marlay House can be explored, along with its walled ornamental and kitchen gardens. The Marlay Craft Centre has a variety of craft workshops, while a market is staged on Saturdays and Sundays.

MINK IN THE WILD

Dundrum was one of the first places in Ireland to get a mink farm, back in 1955, owned by a veterinary surgeon called McDougald. He lived in a big house called Glenville, subsequently demolished for the construction of the Dundrum Shopping Centre. The land behind the house sloped down to the banks of the River Slang, which meant that it was prone to flooding. The mink farm was set up in the grounds of Glenville, but in a great flood during the winter after it was established, the cages housing the mink were swept down the river. The mink managed to escape and their descendants have been living along the River Dodder ever since.

RIVER SLANG

Two streams merge near the recently refurbished family recreation centre at Meadowbrook, Dundrum, to form one river, the Slang, which can be traced back to a holy well at Ticknock in the foothills of the Dublin mountains. This holy well was once regarded as having curative powers for people with eye diseases and up until about 100 years ago, pilgrimages used to take place to this well.

The Slang flows under Ballinteer Road, near Wyckham Park, and joins the slightly larger Ticknock River, which flows through the grounds of Gort Muire and Wesley College. The bridge at Ballinteer once formed part of the boundary between Dundrum and Sandyford parishes, before Ballinteer church was built. Some of the flow of the river was diverted into the reservoir at the old Manor Mill Laundry, where it was used to create power and light. The river then emerges again from under Ballinteer Road.

The river is culverted at the rear of what is now the Dundrum Village Centre and continues near the library. Later it reaches Highfield Park, at Windy Arbour, where there was once a paper mill, powered by the river, that produced high-quality banknote paper for export. Close by the paper mill were about fifty two-roomed cottages, occupied by employees of the mill. After heavy rain, the river rose so much that these cottages were often flooded to a depth of about 30 centimetres. But it wasn't until the bridge at the back of the Nine Arches pub was washed away, together with a cottage on the Milltown side, that the residents of these low-lying cottages were rehoused on higher ground. The River Slang of course still has the power to flood, as was seen in the dramatic scenes in the Dundrum Town Centre in the autumn of 2011, which made the front page of *The Irish Times*. Following torrential rain on Three Rock Mountain in October 2011, the River Slang burst its banks at the millpond near the old castle and flooded the ground floor of the Town Centre to a depth of around 15 centimetres.

Near Milltown cottages, the river goes underground again until it finally joins the River Dodder close to the Luas viaduct, near the entrance to Alexandra College. But in Windy Arbour some of its waters were diverted at Farranboley to power a concrete works, two mills and a tannery.

Until the late 1960s, the River Slang used to be much more of a rural stream and it used to flow through a grassy glen just behind Main Street, but development in recent decades has seen the river become much more confined. However, for most of the distance from just beyond the Dargan Luas bridge at Dundrum to near where it enters the River Dodder, the River Slang is still in the open air.

RURAL TERRACES

Close to the Dargan Luas bridge in Dundrum, on the Dublin side of the road junction, three small terraces off Dundrum Road offer delightful and almost rural vistas well away from the hustle of Dundrum itself and the town centre. These three short roads are called Alexandra Terrace, Magenta Terrace and Victoria Terrace.

THREE WALKING TRAILS
AROUND DUNDRUM

The Dundrum area has three walking trails along what are called Greenways. The first goes from Ballinteer to Stepaside, through Ticknock and across the Three Rock and the Two Rock mountains, extending for over 12½ kilometres. The second trail is much shorter,being just under 5 kilometres. It starts in Clonskeagh and follows the River Dodder, through Milltown to the Rathfarnham Shopping Centre on Butterfield Avenue. The third trail is slightly shorter at 3½ kilometres, starting on Sandyford Road in south Dundrum and following the Slang River, the Wyckham Stream and the Little Dargle River as far as Marlay Park. The river corridor and the Greenway provide a safe haven for many species of fauna and birdlife. Similar Greenways, for walkers and cyclists, are planned throughout the greater Dundrum area in the coming years, to link up parks and public places.

7

PUBS, RESTAURANTS
AND LEISURE

BALALLY PLAYERS

This noted local amateur drama group began life in 1982, when a notice posted by Peter Collier brought the whole concept into being, with the help of other founding members, including Jean Monahan, Karen Carleton and Nora Connolly. Since 1983 it has staged many dramatic productions annually and it uses the Mill Theatre in Dundrum Town Centre for its performances. Most years, it produces one or two full-length shows, a Christmas variety special, a competitive one-act play and longer plays for the festival circuit. There is also a summer Shakespeare production and 'Christmas at Airfield', both performed in this historic house.

The Balally Players began competing on the drama festival circuit in Ireland in the late 1980s and have been doing so ever since. Members have taken plays to Canada, Denmark, France and the United States. In 2009, the Balally Players represented Ireland at the Mondial du Theatre world theatre festival in Monaco. In 2013-14, the chairman of the players was one of its founding members, Karen Carleton.

Full-length productions in recent years have ranged from Martin McDonagh's black-comedy, the *Cripple of Inishmaan*, to Marina Carr's dark tragedy, *By the Bog of Cats*. Classics from the Irish canon have also been performed, such as John B. Keane's *Many Young Men of Twenty* and Sean O'Casey's classic, *The Plough and the Stars*. The group has also brought to audiences lesser performed Irish works, such as Brian Friel's *Aristocrats* and Tom MacIntyre's *The Great Hunger*. Works by American dramatists such as Tennessee Williams have also been presented, including Williams's *The Glass Menagerie*.

The group meets in St Tiernan's Community School on Monday and Wednesday nights, while its typical annual repertoire includes at least two full-length productions, a number of one-act shows and many workshops and social events. Many members describe the Balally Players as being like 'one big family', with the common commitment of staging performances that delight and provoke audiences.

COSGRAVE'S PUB, WINDY ARBOUR

Cosgrave's Windy Arbour House, the predecessor of Ryan's pub in this district, was once a popular hostelry. Occasionally in the early years of the twentieth century, James Cosgrave found himself in court, charged with selling liquor to non bona fide travellers – a rather common offence at that time. Eventually, in 1915, he sold the pub, which also had the Bagatelle Room, a second function room, and adjoining shop, so that he could concentrate on his farming business. Also included in that sale were a bottle washing building, stables and a good cellar, besides six apartments and three adjoining cottages.

DEVENEY'S OFF-LICENCE

This noted off-licence at the crossroads in Dundrum village has been on that corner site since the early 1970s. The original shop was in Rathgar, where it began as a general grocery store, back in 1909. Then in the 1950s, the grandparents of Ruth Deveney, who today runs the Dundrum shop, started selling beer, wine and spirits. She continues to run the Dundrum off-licence, while another one in Rathmines, independent of her shop, is run by a cousin of her father's.

In 2005, the Groceries Order, which had banned the selling of goods below cost price, was abolished and this opened the way for supermarkets to promote offsales of wines, spirits and big boxes of beer. Ruth Deveney says that around eight years ago, the big change came when sales of lagers fell through the floor. Ruth, the fourth generation of Deveneys in the business, said the change in the drinks market forced her to take a close look at how the family business was being run and change accordingly.

Even though Ruth then wasn't a great fan of beer, that's what provided the salvation of the off-licence business, as Deveney's developed a new strategy of selling imported craft beers. Since then, the craft beer market has become a mainstay for this well-known off-licence. Nevertheless, it still sells an impressive array of wines and spirits. The building housing Deveney's has a plaque on its gable elevation showing that it has been around 130 years old, making it one of the oldest buildings on Main Street. It was built in 1880 and had at least nine retail occupiers before Deveney's, including Wine Cellars, one of several who sold alcoholic drinks here. At one stage in the 1920s, the building housed a sub-office to the National Bank in Rathmines, but in those days, Dundrum was so small it couldn't even support one bank, so that a sub-office in what is now Deveney's building only lasted a few months. After the bank closed down, it became a ladies' fashion shop called Vogue. Today, it's all very different, with craft beers the fashion of the age and two banks in the village.

DUBLIN SOUTH FM

The district's community radio station is based in the Dundrum Town Centre, where it has its studios on Level 5. It broadcasts on 93.9FM twelve hours a day, as well as being streamed on the internet. Altogether, it makes close on 100 hours of local programming a week, with the help of around 100 volunteers of all ages and abilities from the local community, whose assistance includes presentation. The station covers the wider Dundrum area, including Ballinteer, Windy Arbour and Stillorgan as well as other slightly more distant districts such as Mount Merrion and Sandyford. It was the first community radio station to go on air back in 1995, licensed by the Broadcasting Authority of Ireland.

The station had started up in Rathfarnham before moving to Dundrum. Before it started, various 'pirate' radio stations broadcast in this part of south Dublin, including South Dublin Radio about 1981 which had a powerful signal. Subsequently, around 1987, another station of the same name set up in what had been the old Pye Radio factory. Then in late 1987, its frequency was taken over by Southside Radio. Dublin South Community Radio started in the early 1980s, based in Dún Laoghaire. In 1988, Dundrum had another 'pirate', operating from a laneway courtyard site just off Main Street and right opposite the Dundrum Shopping Centre. Another local 'pirate' station in 1988 was Zike FM, a very small hobby station operated from Ballinteer.

DUNDRUM BOWL

The bowling alley in what had been the old Pye Radio factory at Dundrum proved popular for a few years, but it closed down in 1993, following flooding on the nearby River Slang. Ironically, the bowling centre in nearby Stillorgan has survived. The old Dundrum Bowl became the first centre in Ireland to install the Quasar computer game system, which still exists today in nine other centres in Ireland. Dundrum Bowl also had Street Fighter, an arcade game, and today people still remember going to Dundrum Bowl in the late 1980s and early 1990s to play Street Fighter and for the rock 'n' bowl sessions on Friday nights. The centre also had a Wally Rabbit play centre for children.

DUNDRUM BRASS AND REED BAND

The original band was founded in 1870 and had its headquarters on Ballinteer Road, not far from what is now Campbell's Corner. One member, Jack Keogh, was reputed to have played at Parnell's funeral in 1891. The band lasted until 1929, when it closed down, but by 1933, it had been revived. Local people collected £450, nearly €28,000 in today's money, to buy new instruments and uniforms.

A Garda superintendent called D.J. Delaney, who came from Dundrum and who was the conductor of the Garda Band at the time, trained the revived band three nights a week. During the shortages of the Second World War emergency, the band closed down, for a second time.

Then in 1983, a campaign aimed at reviving it again got under way, led by Sonny Walsh, William Matthews and a local civil servant and author, Jim Nolan. Between them, they managed to raise nearly £10,000. However, what was described as a 'third generation' revival didn't last.

DUNDRUM MAIN STREET

Main Street has a branch of Leo Burdock's fish and chip shop, as well as Cha, teppanyaki and sushi bar. In the Dundrum Village Centre, the Coffee Gallery is noted for its coffees and meals, while Doyle's food store also has plenty of goodies to be sampled.

DUNDRUM ON ICE

Every October, the 'Dundrum on Ice' rink opens on the town square in the Dundrum Town Centre and remains open until the following January. It gives visitors a great chance to go ice-skating indoors and the experience is enhanced by the terrific sound system and the superb light show. Special offers are provided for groups, while lessons for beginners are also organised.

DUNDRUM LIBRARY

In the 1920s and 1930s, the Carnegie Library in Dundrum was the district's main entertainment centre.

Up on the first floor of the library was an elaborate stage, as well as a kitchen and the facilities were used frequently by groups in the local community for dances, plays and sales of works. In the early 1920s, when the library was less than 10 years old, it was frequently used for concerts organised by Cathal McGarvey and a local organist called Mollie Gallagher. In that same decade, Irish step dancing classes were organised in the library by 'Jem' Byrne, while in the late 1920s, one

Dundrum Brass & Reed Band
Third Generation

Grand Opening Concert
Sunday June 17 1984
in

OUR LADY'S SCHOOL HALL
St. Columbanus Road Windy Arbour
Commencing at 8 p.m.

Tickets   (Children 50p.)   £1.00

particularly memorable theatrical production of *Babes in the Wood* pantomime was performed by the local drama group. The library was also home to the Dundrum Ceili Band, which was known locally as Maureen Boland's Band, as she was the chief pianist and the main organiser.

DUNDRUM RAILWAY TAVERN

This establishment opened in 1854, to coincide with the coming of the railway to Dundrum. Located in the centre of Dundrum it offered breakfast, luncheon and dinner 'at a moment's notice and on the most moderate terms'.

DUNDRUM TOWN CENTRE PUBS

The centre has a couple of pubs, Winters and Ruairi McGuire's. McGuire's pub, under Hamley's toy store, serves a great variety of food. Dundrum Town Centre also has a nightclub called Parker Brown's.

DUNDRUM TOWN CENTRE RESTAURANTS

The town centre has an incredible number of restaurants – forty in all. They include Ananda (Indian cuisine) and Baked (traditional artisan food on Level 3).

Beeftro is in the Pembroke District on ground level outside the main building, while Café Zest is in the House of Fraser store, as its itsa@harveynicholls, part of a popular bagel chain. Harvey Nicholls also has the Rock Bar for cocktails and the Lobster fish and steak house. Cortina's Mexican restaurant in is the Pembroke District, while the Dante pizza place is in the cinema building, along with Eddie Rocket's, KFC, Pizza Hut and TGI Friday's. Douglas and Kaldi has a terrace café on Level 2, along with a restaurant, while Frango's world cuisine is on Level 3. Jamie's Italian restaurant is in the Pembroke District. It opened in 2012 as Jamie Oliver's first Irish restaurant. Another Italian-themed restaurant, L'Officina, by Dunne & Crescenzi, is in the Town Square. The Mao restaurant and Milano's are also in the Town Square. The Siam Thai restaurant is also located there.

Nando's is in the Pembroke District, as is the Counter and the Port House Ibéricos, serving wines and tapas. Wagamama is in this same part of the centre, while completing this round-up of eateries is Yo!, a sushi restaurant, on Level 1.

One of the most enticing restaurants is slightly outside the centre, Roly's, which is based in the eighteenth-century Mill House. Roly's backs on to the pond feature in the centre and is noted for its lunch and dinner menus.

DUNDRUM – TOWN WITH NO HOTELS

Dundrum has a unique distinction for a busy suburb of its size – it hasn't got a hotel of its own, although neighbouring districts like Stillorgan and Sandyford do have excellent hotel facilities. At the time the Dundrum Town Centre was being built, a substantial hotel was planned for Dundrum, but it was never built. That was in 2004, when it was proposed that the 1970s Dundrum Shopping Centre should be demolished. One of the central provisions of that plan was a 105-bedroom luxury hotel, together with three luxury stores, but the whole scheme remained aspirational – it never happened and Dundrum never got its very own modern hotel.

What is now Ryan's Dundrum House pub on Main Street was once called the Dundrum Hotel, but Dundrum hasn't had one for over fifty years now. One of the few luxurious places to stay in Dundrum is Sarah Lafferty's renovated Georgian cottage at Victoria Terrace, a little lane close to the centre of Dundrum. Sarah's luxuriously appointed place has every last comfort for its guests with Sarah herself described as a fabulous and charming hostess. Her breakfast servings, both Irish and Continental, are also highly regarded.

Dundrum also has a few bed and breakfast places, including Dundrum House on Taney Road and Tall Trees on Broadford Hill. The latter offers a suite with sitting room, bedroom, with double and single bed, and an en suite wet room (bathroom in old fashioned terminology). In neighbouring Rathfarnham, Grange Wood B&B previously offered six guest rooms, but has since been sold.

DUNDRUM VILLAGE FLOWER AND GARDEN CLUB

This long-established club reflects a popular pastime in the district – gardening – and it hosts regular weekly meetings in the Gort Muire Centre in Ballinteer. Here many varied gardening and related topics are discussed and presented.

GLENCULLEN DUNDRUM MUSICAL AND DRAMATIC SOCIETY

Founded close on forty years ago in the Glencullen area in the foothills of the Dublin mountains, the Glencullen Dundrum Musical and Dramatic Society has since extended its geographical coverage and now has members from many areas of Dublin. They produce and take part in a wide range of musicals and drama productions annually. Among the well over thirty drama productions have been *The Field* and *Dancing at Lughnasa*, while more than twenty musicals, including *My Fair Lady*, have also been produced. Two of the longest serving members of the society died in 2013. George Ward, who was 78, was chairman more than once and took part in numerous theatrical and musical productions. He was always quick with a joke. Another long-time member was Tommy Dargan. He had joined the society in 1986 and had taken part in numerous shows.

GOAT GRILL, GOATSTOWN

What has been known in recent years as the Goat Grill, at the crossroads in Goatstown, owned by Charlie Chawke, was once called Traynor's. Over a century ago, when Goatstown was a small isolated hamlet, the pub was owned by P.A. Dickson. A niece of the owner married a barman called Traynor and in due course, the pub was renamed Traynor's.

GROCERY BARS

In the old days in Dundrum most premises also had an adjoining grocery shop, as was the case with what is now Uncle Tom's Cabin. Very often, there was very little distinction between the two sides of the business and on busy Saturday nights, it was commonplace for a barmen (no barwomen in those days) to pull a pint and leave it to settle, then move a very short distance to weigh out a couple of pounds of flour for another customer. This common ground, between groceries and liquor, began to disappear in the 1930s.

GYMS

These days gyms are essential centres for leisure activities and today the Dundrum area has around twenty such facilities. Leading facilities include the Dundrum Sports and Leisure Centre. The Rock Fitness Centre, directly opposite the Dundrum Town Centre, has three floors in its gym. Other gyms include Fitworks in Balally, Meadowbrooks in Ballinteer and Body Fitness in the Rockfield Centre at Balally. The Dundrum Town Centre itself has Educogym, while just off Main Street in Dundrum is Curves, aimed specifically at female users.

MEADOWBROOK BOARDING HOUSE

In the early nineteenth century, this was one of the best-known boarding houses in Dundrum, being very popular with people who came to stay from the nearby city of Dublin to avail of the pure country air in Dundrum. Owned and run by Mary Hughes, it advertised extensively at that time. Two of its attributes were excellent stabling and a selection of coaching horses. As with similar tourist establishments in Dundrum at that time, Meadowbrook made much of the fact that respectable ladies and gentlemen went to the area to recuperate in its pure air. An essential part of that cure, as served at Meadowbrook, was goat's milk, considered ideal for people with consumption. It was comparatively expensive at around threepence for a quart jug. But it wasn't served during the month of August, because it became very thick in the heat. In 1813, a Dublin morning newspaper carried an advertisement for Meadowbrook, which read: 'The second whey (made from goat's milk) having commenced, Ladies and Gentlemen are respectively reminded that there are a few vacancies in the House; the accommodation will be found agreeable, and terms very much reduced-Respectable society in the House'. All very different from today's strident advertising for package holidays!

MILL THEATRE

Based in the Town Square of the Dundrum Town Centre, this high-specification, state-of-the-art theatre complex was opened in May

2006 by the then President of Ireland, Mary McAleese. Castlethorn Construction, which developed and built the centre, made a community contribution of over €10 million when it constructed the theatre. The main auditorium has capacity for an audience of 207, while the smaller, complementary Maureen O'Hara Theatre, named after one of Ireland's greatest film actresses, is a more intimate studio space for more experimental productions. The theatre also has an all-important bar, open before, during and after performances and houses the Drama League of Ireland's offices and library.

The origins of the theatre date back to 1998, when three people representing local cultural organisations met with Joe O'Reilly of Castlethorn and his architects and project managers. Those three people were Karen Carleton from the Balally Players, John D. Byrne and Michael Doyle of the Sandyford Little Theatre. Over the following five years, public meetings were held at Airfield and in the Taney Parish Centre, in which all local cultural organisations took part. From those meetings, the board of the Dundrum Theatre Management Company emerged and it is this company that today runs the theatre. It's a limited company with charitable status.

As for financing, the theatre complex is mostly self-financing but it also has limited funding from Dún Laoghaire-Rathdown County

Council. The theatre has become a focal point for community gatherings and it's a home for local theatrical groups and stage schools, helping make Dundrum Town Centre a beating heart for the community of Dundrum and district.

Under its first manager, Stephen Faloon (who went on to become the general manager of the Bord Gáis Energy Theatre in Dublin), the theatre has led excellence and innovation within the performing arts, supported local amateur companies and other groups and provides a meeting space for local and national firms.

MOVIES@DUNDRUM

The Dundrum Town Centre has its own multiplex cinema, with a total of twelve screens showing the latest film releases. In addition, it also has a VIP suite, with extra luxury seating, and this is also used for corporate events. During the summer months, the centre also does 'Movies in the Open', free film screenings in Pembroke Square.

It's a very different kind of cinema to the original picture house in Dundrum, the Odeon, which opened in 1942 and lasted until 1967.

MYLER'S MIX

Thomas Myler is a well-known media personality living in Dundrum (Ailesbury Grove). He covers an unusual mix of topics, including boxing and showbiz and he is currently compiling and writing a history of the much-loved Theatre Royal in Dublin city centre, which closed down in 1962.

ODEON CINEMA

During the 1930s and 1940s, Dublin, and indeed towns and cities throughout Ireland, had a rash of new cinemas, as the introduction of talkies popularised the new medium, from the early 1930s onwards. Dundrum was no exception. The Odeon Cinema was located on Dundrum Road at Rosemount, where the Apollo Building is now situated.

A cinema entrepreneur called Robert Graves Kirkham built the cinema. It was a single-screen operation and on each side of the screen were dais-like structures that turned blue and pink before and after the performance. The cinema could seat 750 people and below it was an underground park for 500 bicycles, the popular mode of transport in those days. At the front of the cinema were two big windows. One was used by a small shop, while the other was used to advertise forthcoming attractions.

The cinema showed all kinds of popular releases and the cost of a ticket ranged from an economical eightpence up to one shilling and fourpence. Apart from films, the Odeon was widely used to stage live performances by local artistes, who put on all kinds of variety shows. The Odeon closed down on 31 May 1959 and was sold the following year to the Apollo group, which reopened it on 12 April 1961, under a new name, the Apollo. It continued to present both films and stage shows for another six years, until it finally closed on 26 February 1967, due to steadily declining audiences.

After the Irish national television service, Telefís Éireann, started, on the last day of December 1961, the number of suburban cinemas went into drastic decline. The movies@dundrum multiplex in the Dundrum Town Centre is one of the few new suburban cinemas left. In 1987, the old Apollo building was converted into retail and office space and it remains that way today, but still called the Apollo Building. The service station in front became a mecca for motorists, at one time selling Jet brand petrol.

RYAN'S DUNDRUM HOUSE

This busy pub on Main Street in Dundrum has been trading since the late nineteenth century, although the present owner, Paddy Ryan, is unsure of the date of its construction. His father, also Patrick, had bought the premises in the mid-1960s and moved out to the then country village of Dundrum from the pub he had previously owned at Islandbridge. As Paddy notes, when the family arrived in Dundrum, the place was still very quiet and undeveloped, but by 1967-68, the housing boom in the area started and the 1970s saw a huge amount of house building. At that stage, he remembers that it was all open land at the back of Simpson's Hospital. In more recent times, Paddy remembers well the big snow in January 1982, when Main Street in Dundrum was completely blocked. Neither buses nor any other vehicle could get through.

At the side of the pub on Main Street can be seen a bricked up gateway that once led to stables. The pub had originally been built as a hotel and horses were stabled here so that guests could be transported by coach. The main staircase in the building led to the two upper floors, which had a total of twelve rooms for guests. At an earlier stage, the pub was owned by the Clarke family who also owned what was then the Swallow pub, now the Eagle, just along the street. But by the late 1950s, the pub was owned by a man called J.V. Murphy and its name was the Dundrum Hotel, clear evidence of its earlier existence.

In the past three or four decades, the pub has often attracted customers who were RTÉ celebrities, such as Charles Mitchel, the TV newsreader, who lived in Dundrum, and Seán MacReamoinn, the RTÉ presenter. Another character from the national broadcasting station who also frequented the pub when he was living on Sandyford Road, was Gene Martin, a well-known producer in RTÉ, described by Paddy Ryan as a 'great character'.

These days, in Ryan's Dundrum House, the smaller bar has been kept as the more old-fashioned one, with lots of old photos and old memorabilia, with even an old wireless set. The main bar does a significant food trade and lots of sports events are shown on television, while Friday and Saturday nights see music sessions.

Paddy Ryan's father died in 1980 and the family went on to buy what is now Ryan's pub in Windy Arbour in 1981. It too has an interesting history, dating from the mid-nineteenth century. Previously, an alleyway of single-storey rural dwellings had been on the site and when the pub was being built, the builder simply removed the roofs from the cottages and left the rest of the buildings in place. Today, in the cellars of the pub, the remains of these old houses can still be seen.

SANDYFORD AND SOUTH DUBLIN PLAYERS

This amateur drama group now attracts members from all over south Dublin and beyond to take part in its many performances.

SINGAPORE GARDENS

One of the very exotic restaurants to open in the Dundrum area, forty years ago, the Singapore Gardens was at 15 Main Street, Dundrum. That site is now occupied by the Permanent TSB bank building.

TANEY DRAMA SOCIETY

Reflecting the strong interest in amateur drama and musicals in the Dundrum area, the Taney Drama Society has been going strong since 1991, producing a wide variety of drama performances. Smaller scale performances take place in the Taney Parish Centre, while larger productions are staged in the Mill Theatre in Dundrum Town Centre.

TELEVISION SCREENS IN DUNDRUM TOWN CENTRE

The Dundrum Town Centre has DTV, short for Dundrum Television. It uses three large screens in high-profile locations, on Level 3 overlooking Frangos, the Mill Pond and the foyer for the cinema building. Until 2013, RTÉ was providing the content, including streamed news and sports news, but the facility is now run by Communicorp. Tenants can and do advertise on these screens, as well as providing content, especially the fashion retailers in the centre. The screens are also used for showing big sporting events, such as football matches.

THE CORNER HOUSE PUB, WINDY ARBOUR

Also known as Kynes, this long-established pub, trading for over a century, was previously known as The Nine Arches pub (after what is now the Luas bridge at Milltown), while before that again, it was known as J.D.'s Corner House and as the Mill Race.

THE COUNTY CLUB

Until the late 1980s, the County Club on Churchtown Road Upper was a popular drinking and dining venue, while cabaret performances were staged in the adjoining Braemor Rooms. This used to be a very popular venue for live performances that took place while patrons enjoyed a meal. After the pub and the Braemor Rooms closed, the property reinvented itself as Faces disco and nightclub. These days, the premises is used as Rodeo Joe's nightclub.

THE EAGLE

What is today the Eagle, with its adjacent bar called the Nest, was once called the Swallow. The actual building housing the Eagle Bar dates back to the early nineteenth century, since it was marked on an 1837 map of the area. It is delightfully reminiscent of an earlier era, with its wooden panelling and old-fashioned bar. Its previous owners include the Clarke family and the Dwyer brothers. Today it is owned by Padraig McWeeney of Dundrum Taverns.

THE WILLOWS, WYCKHAM PARK

One of the area's newer pubs, The Willows is, unsurprisingly, in Willows Road in Wyckham Park, within walking distance of the Dundrum Town Centre. The main bar has a real fire, as well as wifi and an off-licence.

WINDY ARBOUR'S YUKON GOLD

One old-time pub in Windy Arbour, Devancys, was bought by a man called Devaney with the proceeds of the several years he spent prospecting in the Yukon. Some of his fortune was in gold dust, while the rest was in diamonds. He had no faith in the banks or paper money, so he carried his worldly fortune in leather bags tied around his waist. The bar owner was in the habit of going into town once a month to get stociously drunk and on one of those occasions, when he was returning home, he was stopped by two youths at Milltown bridge, who demanded a light. Devancy produced a match and when one of the youths asked what they would strike it on, the pub owner promptly produced his gun. 'Strike it on that' was his riposte, at which the two youths disappeared, hastily.

UNCLE TOM'S CABIN

Just on the Dublin side of the Dargan Luas bridge junction at Dundrum, Uncle Tom's Cabin on Dundrum Road has been a fixture of the area for over 170 years. It started off in 1842 as a grocery shop with a small bar, owned by a man called John Murphy. The pub then became the Cyclists' Rest and Tea Gardens. In 1888, it was bought by James Collins, grandfather of the present owner, Tony

Collins, which means it has been in the Collins family for close on 130 years.

James Collins had been born in the gate lodge of St Columbanus' College, nearby, and his first job was as a messenger boy in a long-extinct pub in Dundrum that lost its licence because gambling took place on the premises. Then he went to work at the Yellow House in Rathfarnham, before becoming manager of the Dolphin Hotel in East Essex Street, Dublin, which closed down forty years ago. Eventually, he became owner of The Fleet in Fleet Street, opposite the side entrance of the old *Irish Times* building.

One day in 1888, he attended a pub auction in Dublin, having decided he wanted to move to the suburbs. He had wanted to buy the Horse Show House in Ballsbridge, but he was late and by the time he arrived at the auctioneers, that pub had been sold. He then made a successful bid for the next pub that came up, the one owned by John Murphy in Dundrum. After the sale, when he was trying to decide on a new name for the pub, his wife looked at the book James was reading and said: 'Uncle Tom's Cabin – that's what we'll call it'. It has stuck with that name ever since.

Until the Collins takeover, the pub had been single storey, but James Collins had the upper storeys built in 1901. His wife insisted on the large front windows upstairs, so that she could keep an eye out up and down the road outside. In those days, the pub was very much in the country. His son Edward, father of Tony Collins, the present owner, was born in 1901. But going back well over a century, when what is now Uncle Tom's Cabin, was a grocery shop as much as a pub, the place was as well known for its blend of tea (which it sold for around two shillings eightpence a pound), as for its beer.

In early 1923, the police barracks in Dundrum was burned down. The local IRA men responsible had collected lots of empty beer bottles from the back of the pub to fill with petrol and use as Molotov cocktails. James Collins insisted that before the IRA men took away the bottles, they remove the labels showing the name of his pub. In those earlier days, the pub had stables at the back and a couple of horses were kept for pulling the carts used to deliver groceries from the shop. Five years after that IRA attack in Dundrum, Uncle Tom's Cabin had another startling event, when just before Christmas 1928 a gas explosion blew out all the windows in the pub.

The present owner of the pub, Tony Collins, eventually took over from his father. Tony started as a young lad working in the pub in 1953. He remembers vividly after Guinness withdrew its horse-drawn drays and replaced them with big lorries, the driver and helper on one of those lorries delivering to the pub often put oil on the bonnet of the lorry in the heat of summer. They then bought rashers and eggs from the pub and while they were continuing their rounds, used to fry them on the bonnet of the lorry! Tony Collins also remembers the old cinema in Dundrum in the 1950s, close to the pub, called the Odeon, which eventually became the Apollo Building, with the adjacent Apollo filling station.

Over the years, Tony Collins has made many improvements to the pub, including substantial refurbishments around 1970. In the 1960s and 1970s, one celebrity customer who quite often dropped into the pub was Eamonn Andrews, the Dublin-born TV presenter who was also closely involved in setting up the Irish television service at the end of 1961. Today, the pub is also known for its food trade at lunchtime and for its music sessions. The area around the pub has changed, as has everywhere in Dundrum. In the old days, there were two public lavatories close to the railway station, but they are long gone. Beside the railway bridge, Terry Nolan ran a forge, now disappeared, as is the old bookie's shop, although the ruins of that are still in place.

WINDY ARBOUR PLAYGROUND

One of the longest running community campaigns for leisure facilities ended in 2014. Residents of Windy Arbour had been campaigning for twenty years for a playground in Windy Arbour and it finally opened in May 2014.

8

WELL-KNOWN RESIDENTS

FRANK AIKEN

This familiar political figure was very well known in the Dundrum area and from 1928 lived on his Three Rock Farm at Sandyford until his death in 1983. Originally from County Armagh, he had been a prominent figure in the old IRA in the border area, and in 1923, became the IRA chief of staff. Under his leadership, the IRA laid down its arms at the end of the Civil War that year. In 1926, he was a founding father of the Fianna Fáil party and remained a senior figure for the rest of his life. As a cabinet minister, he was best known for being Minister for External Affairs. The housing development built on his former lands after his death was named Aiken's Village.

NIALL ANDREWS

He was a highly respected political figure in the Dundrum area, serving as a Fianna Fáil TD for Dublin South from 1977 to 1987. Andrews was also an MEP for Dublin from 1984 to 2004. He spent a total of thirty-seven years in politics, but before he went into politics he was a presentation director in RTÉ television from 1963 until 1977. He was a political campaigner long before they became popular and campaigned on behalf of groups searching for justice such as the Birmingham Six. He also had excellent contacts throughout the Middle East but the continent that really appealed to him was Africa.

Niall was a son of Todd Andrews, a long-time resident of Dundrum, as was David Andrews, who served for a time as Foreign Minister. Niall's son, Chris, was a long-serving member of Fianna Fáil, but is now with Sinn Féin. Niall Andrews died in 2006, aged 69. He was survived by his wife Bernadette, his son Chris and his daughters Niamh and Kate.

CHRISTOPHER STEPHEN 'TODD' ANDREWS

Acquiring his nickname Todd because of his resemblance to an English comic strip hero called Alonzo Todd, Andrews came from a poor background in Summerhill in Dublin's north inner city, where he was born in 1901. At the age of 15 he joined the Irish Volunteers in time for the Easter Rising and went on to become an active IRA member during the 1919-1921 War of Independence. He took the republican side during the 1922-23 Civil War and was then interned until 1924.

When the first Fianna Fáil government came to power in 1932, he was put to work in charge of turf or peat development. He had worked first with the Irish Tourist Association, then with the Electricity Supply Board (ESB), before being put in charge of turf development.

In 1946, when Bord na Móna was set up, he became its first managing director. In 1958 he was made chairman of the national transport company CIÉ and it was under his chairmanship of this company that the old Harcourt Street railway line, which ran through Dundrum, was closed down on 1 January 1959. It was one of many controversial railway closures at that time, made because CIÉ was losing so much money. He used to say that the Harcourt Street line was only used by Freemasons and solicitors going into town.

After he became chairman of the RTÉ Authority in 1966, a job that lasted until 1970. He was always a person of colourful language, which he put to good effect in his 2001 biography, *Dublin Made Me*.

Todd Andrews lived for many years in Taney, close to Dundrum village. His first wife, Mary, died in 1967 and he married again, this time to his principal secretary in CIÉ, Joyce Duffy. She died in 2008 and was survived by her stepdaughter Catherine, mother of Ryan Tubridy, the RTÉ presenter. Todd Andrews himself died in 1985 at the age of 85. One of his sons, Niall, who became an MEP, died in 2006, while David is now retired, having once been a Minister for Foreign Affairs. The Andrews family was always staunchly Fianna Fáil, but one of his sons, Chris, who was once a Fianna Fáil TD, is now a Sinn Féin councillor for Pembroke South Dock on Dublin city council.

FRANCIS AND JOHN BRENNAN

In the late 1960s and early 1970s, two schoolboys whose family home was in the Ballaly Drive area, gave little inclination that years later, both would be famous on television. Francis Brennan bought the five-star Park Hotel in Kenmare, County Kerry in 1986 and has since built it up into one of the country's leading luxury hotels. His younger brother John was made general manager of the hotel in 1994. Both have become household names on television, including with the series of *At Your Service* programmes on RTÉ Television, troubleshooting in the hospitality industry and fronted by both of the brothers. It first aired in 2008.

SEAMUS BRENNAN

For long one of the most popular TDs in Dublin South, Seamus Brennan was a Galwegian with a keen interest in politics. At the age of 24, he was the youngest ever general secretary of Fianna Fáil and he introduced many aspects of US political promotion into Irish politics. He was made a senator in 1977. In 1981 he entered the Dáil for the first time, when he was elected as a TD for Dublin South. He also served as a minister and Michael O'Leary of Ryanair says that Seamus Brennan was the best transport minister the country has ever had.

He also had a spell as chief whip for his party, where his genial manner came in useful. In 2004, when Bertie Ahern was Taoiseach, many of Seamus Brennan's constituents felt that he had been 'shafted' when he was moved from his transport job to become Minister for Social Welfare. He fought his last general election campaign in 2007, despite being diagnosed with cancer, which meant he could no longer canvass, but topped the poll in Dublin South. He died on 9 July 2008, aged just 60. Large numbers of people attended his funeral and burial at St Nahi's in Dundrum. He was survived by his wife Ann and six children. One of his children, Shay, was elected a councillor in Dundrum in May 2014.

PAUL CAMPBELL

One of Dundrum's best-known characters, Paul Cambell, who was born in 1948, runs his shoe repairing business at Campbell's Corner at 14 Main Street in Dundrum. Paul started in the shop when he was 15 and eventually took over the business from his father, Jack, who in turn had taken it over from his father, Michael.

MAIN STREET,
AND BALLINTEER ROAD. DUNDRUM.
Co. DUBLIN, *July 28th* 192 3

M~rs~ *Nolan*

Pembroke Cottages

Dr. to **CAMPBELL,**

HIGH-CLASS BOOT REPAIRER.

Aug 25th Piece on Boy's Book		9
Sept 4th Pair Heels 1 Sole	3	6
Dec 1st Gents Soled-Heeled x	6	6
	10	9
By allowance on ...		
Gents Repair x 3/=	3/	-
	7	9

Paid

[signature]

The shop was opened about 1900, in Michael's name, because Patrick, Michael's brother, was the master shoemaker and mender in the asylum at Windy Arbour. The original Campbell shoe shop had been in Parliament Street, in Dublin city centre, going back to 1849. Paul's son, also Paul, worked in the Dundrum shop for twenty-six years but now has his own shoe repair business in Enniscorthy, County Wexford. Campbell's is the last of the old-time traders left on Main Street in Dundrum, by Paul's reckoning.

Both Paul and his wife Florrie are well-known personalities in Dundrum and Paul is a previous Mayor of Dundrum. In 2011, media arts students from the Dublin Institute of Technology made an excellent DVD about Paul Campbell and Campbell's Corner, describing it as the last traditional shop in Dundrum. Paul points out that at the time the Dundrum Town Centre was being built, many improvements were promised for Dundrum, including street furniture and trees for Main Street. They were delayed because of the recession but he hopes that now, with the economy improving, these ideas might now be revived.

WILLIAM DARGAN

In the later part of his life the great railway pioneer William Dargan lived at his residence Mount Anville, now the renowned second-level fee-paying girls school of the same name. Born in Carlow in 1799,

Dargan trained as an engineer and initially worked in Wales on the construction of the railway to Holyhead. Returning to Ireland, he became an entrepreneur, connected with the building of almost every railway line in Ireland. He proposed Ireland's first railway, from Westland Row to Kingstown, now Dún Laoghaire, which opened in 1834. He went on to connect Dublin with Belfast, Cork and Galway. He made great sums of money for himself by leasing out the railways he had built and from his shrewd investments. But he was a liberal employee, known to those who worked for him as the man with his hand in his pocket.

Originally, he lived in Raheny but in later life he acquired the house and estate at Mount Anville. He also had a town house at 2 Fitzwilliam Square, in Dublin. Not only did he design the railway station at Dundrum, but he built for himself a luxurious railway carriage, which is now at the Ulster Folk and Transport Museum at Cultra, near Belfast. He was also very involved in financing and creating the Dublin Industrial Exhibition of 1853 on Leinster Lawn, then owned by the Royal Dublin Society. Queen Victoria came to Dublin for that exhibition. Dargan went up the tower at Mount Anville, from where he could see the Queen's ship sailing into Kingstown Harbour. Queen Victoria took tea with Dargan at Mount Anville and offered him a baronetcy, which he politely declined. For that exhibition, many paintings were assembled and they formed the basis of the National Gallery of Ireland, built close by Leinster Lawn in 1859-60. Dargan is forever associated with the National Gallery and his statue stands outside.

In 1866, while he was out riding his horse along the Stillorgan Road, a maid shook bedsheets out of a house window that frightened his horse. Dargan had a bad fall, from which he never recovered. He had never delegated work, so his business interests fell apart very quickly. He sold Mount Anville and retreated to his house in Fitzwilliam Square, but died there on 6 February 1867.

DR LIAM DILLON DIGBY

Dr Dillon Digby, who succeeded his father as managing director of Pye Ireland, lived during the later part of his life at the Mill House, which is now Roly Saul's restaurant. At that stage, he was the manager of the First National Building Society office at 7 Main Street, Dundrum. Before moving to the Mill House, he had lived at a house called The Boulders in Sydenham Road, Dundrum. Dr Dillon Digby is recalled as a genial man, blessed with a great sense of humour.

DUNDRUM'S CHARACTERS

In the old days, going back before the Second World War, Dundrum was peopled not only with wealthy aristocrats and rich upper-class families living in the many big houses that once dotted the district, but also by a rich and stimulating mixture of working-class characters, who added to the gaiety of the place.

One such person was the 'Bird' Flanagan, who played practical jokes all over south County Dublin, not just Dundrum. One of the most famous stories about him concerns the time he arrived in Dundrum by train, then took a horse-drawn cab to a large, remote farm beyond Ballinteer (the farm has long since been submerged under a housing estate, but in those days, it was a very rural setting). Flanagan knocked on the door of the farmhouse and told the farmer that he was an inspector from the Department of Agriculture. He told the farmer that having inspected the cow houses, certain structural alterations would need to be carried out. Flanagan said that he would call again in three weeks' time to make sure the work had been done. The unfortunate farmer, who had never checked Flanagan's credentials, duly demolished some of the roofs and walls of the cow houses. A little uncertain as to what he should build to succeed them, he rang the Department of Agriculture in Dublin city centre, only to realise that he had been duped, and very expensively at that!

On another occasion Flanagan arrived at Dundrum station and once again engaged a horse-drawn cab, driven by the same man as in the previous episode, 'Struggler' Burke. This time the journey was to a remote pub in the foothills of the Dublin mountains. Flanagan ordered a glass of the publican's best whiskey, then when it arrived, poured the spirits into a bottle and pocketed it. The publican sensed trouble and told Flanagan that the whiskey had been poured by mistake from a bottle of medicine for sick animals. Flanagan then announced that he was an excise inspector but the publican settled the matter by giving Flanagan a £5 note, a very substantial sum of money in those days, equal to a fortnight's wages for many people. Flanagan gave the cab driver a substantial tip from the fiver while they enjoyed several free pints on the house.

Another eccentric character, sometimes seen in Dundrum, was Joe Edelstein, who loved to call out the fire brigade, complimenting them when they arrived. Before telephones came into general use, fire alarms were located in small metal boxes with glass windows on top of a metre-high pole. When a window in the box was broken, it activated the alarm in the fire station.

One character in particular was a favourite in Dundrum – the 'Ladder' Young, who stood nearly 2 metres tall. He was seen one day pushing an old pram along Main Street in Dundrum, and knowing his reputation as a very reliable tipster, scanned through the racing pages in the morning newspapers. True to form, a horse called Perambulator was running that day, so there was a frantic rush to the bookies. The horse came in at three to one, so Young's reputation was made, at least for the moment.

William Oakes was perhaps the most colourful character in the Dundrum of old. A Church of Ireland man, he lived in an imposing gate lodge at Tawney Park in Churchtown and was the custodian of Churchtown Graveyard. In the mornings, he had little to do except walk as far as Clarke's grocery shop in Main Street, Dundrum, make himself comfortable on a sack of sugar and then sip the glass of whiskey that was waiting for him. He quite often wore a check suit and a straw hat, besides having a rose or a pansy in his buttonhole. An ecumenist well before the term was fashionable, he attended funerals of all denominations.

When it came to his own funeral, he appointed the two local blacksmiths, John Nolan (father of Dundrum author Jim Nolan) and John Hanlon, both Catholics, as pallbearers, together with two Protestant dairymen, Willie Young and Sam Ferguson. His wishes were duly carried out.

The Dundrum area in the 1920s and 1930s had a plethora of other great characters, each of whom had his own particular nickname, whether it was Scorcher Morrin, Snailer Nolan or Lobber Brennan – well over two dozen in fact. Without exception, they were all men. These days, the characters and the jokers of yesteryear have long since gone to their eternal reward, never to be replaced.

BRENDA FRICKER

The well-known Brenda Fricker actress was born and brought up in Windy Arbour, almost beside the walls of the asylum. She was born in 1945. Her father Desmond had worked in the Department of Agriculture and then became a journalist with *The Irish Times*. Through her father's good offices, she got her first job at that newspaper, as assistant to the art editor. She had hoped to graduate to the reporting staff, but a chance film role when she was 19 changed her life. She got a small, uncredited part in a film called *Of Human Bondage*, based on a work by Somerset Maugham.

After that, her acting career took off. She starred in Ireland's first television soap, *Tolka Row*, then started in *Coronation Street* in

1977. Her most noted film role was as Christy Brown's mother in *My Left Foot*, which won her an Oscar for best supporting actress in 1996. She went on to act in many more films, as well as television and the theatre, including the National Theatre and the Royal Court Theatre, both in London. Among her most recent work has been the 2013 TV series, *Forgive Me*. She now lives in the Liberties in Dublin.

PATRICK FUNGE

Patrick Funge and his wife Josephine were leading lights in Dublin theatre and lived at Windy Arbour for many years. Patrick and Josephine founded the highly regarded Lantern Theatre in Dublin in 1957, which lasted until 1975. Patrick's cousin, the well-known portrait painter and teacher Paul Funge, founded the Gorey Arts Centre and annual arts festival in 1970 and Patrick and Josephine often brought theatrical productions to the festival. Patrick died in October 2013.

CANON WILLIAM MONK GIBBON

Born in 1864, he was the rector of Taney Parish from 1901 until his death in 1935. He was responsible for the most recent restoration of St Nahi's church in 1910 and he is buried there. He was also responsible for installing some of the fine stained-glass windows. He and his family were interred near the entrance to the graveyard. His son, William Monk Gibbon, was a distinguished writer and poet, often referred to as the 'Grand Old Man of Irish Letters'. He died in 1987. William was also a friend of the Yeats sisters, Elizabeth and Susan, very involved in the Cuala Press in Dundrum.

TOM GLENNON

A well-known journalist in Dublin, Tom Glennon lived in Dundrum. He came from Athlone, where his father, John E. Glennon, was once the editor of the *Westmeath Independent*. Tom worked in various regional newspapers, including the *Clare Champion* in Ennis, and he had a fund of hilarious stories about working in local newspapers. In time, he came to Dublin where he worked for *The Irish Times*, rising to the post of chief-sub-editor. Tom died on 15 February 2009.

His funeral was at Holy Cross church in Dundrum. He was survived by his wife Pat and his two children.

SEÁN LEMASS

The best-known political figure in the Dundrum area, Séan Lemass was first elected to the Dublin South constituency in 1924, as a Sinn Féin candidate. In the 1927 general election, he topped the poll for the then new Fianna Fáil party and served the people of the constituency until 1948, when Dublin South was abolished. Lemass then moved to Dublin South Central, which encompassed Dundrum, and served there until he retired from the Dáil in 1969. Lemass, who was Taoiseach from 1959 until 1966, was widely regarded as the 'father of modern Ireland'.

Other early TDs in the area included Constance Marckiewicz, Sinn Féin, in 1921. In 1938, Robert Briscoe was elected for Fianna Fáil for the first time and subsequently became a Lord Mayor of Dublin. In 1943, a noted Fine Gael TD was elected for the first time, Maurice Dockrell.

The old Dublin South constituency was revived in 1980 and in the first election after that, in 1981, Alan Shatter was elected and remains a local TD. He was a controversial minister, for Justice Equality and Defence, and stepped down in May 2014.

Other well-known TDs in the area in recent years have included Niall Andrews, John Kelly, Nuala Fennell, Liz O'Donnell and Tom Kitt. The Green Party made its first breakthrough here with Roger Garland, but in the 2011 general election, Green Party leader Eamon Ryan lost his seat. Shane Ross was elected as an independent in that election, as was Peter Mathews, who went on to become independent of Fine Gael, while Alex White was elected for Labour and became a junior minister.

After the high-profile Seámus Brennan died in July 2008, a by-election was held eleven months later. One of his sons, Shay, ran for election but came third, with 9,250 votes. George Lee from RTÉ took the seat for Fine Gael, but disillusioned, left politics after nine months in the Dáil. He returned to RTÉ and is now the station's agricultural and environmental correspondent.

JOHN G. LENNON

John, who lives in Frankfort Park, off Dundrum Road, close to the Dargan Luas bridge, is well-known in the district as the founder of the Dundrum & District History Society and the person who keeps the society going. Over the years he has made many presentations on numerous aspects of local history, such as Dundrum Castle. In 2014, he talked about the 100-year-old history of the library in Dundrum, opened as a Carnegie Library in 1914. His society has regular weekly meetings in Dom Marmion House in Sandyford. Other local history societies in the Dundrum area include the one covering Kilmacud and Stillorgan. The Ballinteer Family History Society closed down nearly ten years ago.

SEÁN MACREAMOINN

Born in Birmingham in 1921 of a Wexford father, Sean MacReamoinn's family came back to Ireland when he was just two years of age. Seán worked for the Department of External Affairs – now the Department of Foreign Affairs and Trade – from 1944 to 1947. However, he soon found his niche in life, in broadcasting, joining Radio Éireann shortly afterwards. In his earlier years, he also wrote pantomime scripts for the Abbey Theatre. He spent much of his first few years in radio on the road with Seamus Ennis, touring the country to record folk music and stories. Later he became a religious correspondent and when Vatican II was taking place in Rome in the early 1960s, it was he who described for people in Ireland exactly what was being proposed.

Seán, who lived in Dundrum for many years, was a passionate advocate of traditional Irish music around the country and was a co-founder of the Merriman School in County Clare. In his later years, he would often attend Mass in Holy Cross church in Dundrum, then go to the small bookshop that Liz Meldon ran, collect his book orders and finally repair to Ryan's pub across the road for a liquid lunch. A very entertaining and versatile speaker, he once said, memorably, in his later years, that he was like the census, broken down by age, religion and sex. Seán died on 17 January 2007, survived by his wife and three children.

JOHN MELLON

John Mellon was one of the Mellon family who once ran a garage of the same name on Main Street in Dundrum. The garage was close to the crossroads in Dundrum, opposite the Eagle Bar, with Leverett & Frye (now Ladbrokes) and Campbell's shoe repairs on the other corner. The business had been started by an earlier John Mellon in the late nineteenth century. Later, during the 1930s and 1940s, four Mellon brothers, Johnny, Joseph, Paddy and Dick all worked in the garage, which thrived during the Second World War. Paddy, who was also a local taxi driver, was the family member most involved in the garage.

John Mellon, son of Joseph, had been born had been born in 1940. After third-level education he graduated from UCD and started working for the *Daily Telegraph* in London on the marketing side. He died in 2008, just after he had privately published his memoirs on growing up in Dundrum. His widow Patricia, whom he had married in London in 1965, now lives in County Wexford.

MEN OF THE MOUNTAINS

Many of the long-established traditional families living in the Sandyford-Barnacullia area were close knit, especially around Barnacullia and Ticknock. It used to be said by one woman living in this area years ago that 'hit one of us and hit us all'. These communities were so closely knit and inter-married that someone from Dublin, or elsewhere in Ireland, let alone the world, would be considered a 'blow in' for the first twenty years of their residency. But in the last couple of decades, many more people from outside the area have come to live, particularly in Dundrum and Sandyford.

In Sandyford, the most common family name for many years was Doyle, which is derived from the Norse word for a 'dark foreigner'. Some historians believe there was a Norse settlement in Sandyford, while Balally was named after a Danish king who became St Olaf.

In the Ticknock area, the main family name is Kelly. A century and more ago, when the main shopping of the week was done on Saturday nights – the shops often stayed open until 11 p.m. that night – the Doyles from Sandyford and the Kellys from Ticknock came to Dundrum's Main Street to do their shopping. The Doyles used to park all their carts along the side of Main Street, while the Kellys preferred Ballinteer Road. After the shopping was done, the drivers of these carts would repair to one of the local hostelries for suitable refreshments, so much so that they were incapable of driving their carts home. Fortunately, the horses had an uncanny knack of finding their own way home, which they did with great accuracy and without any help from the sozzled drivers.

CHARLES MITCHEL

The first newsreader on Telefís Éireann, the Irish television service that went on the air on the last day of December 1961, Charles Mitchel, was a long-time resident of Dundrum with his wife Betty Stubbs, whom he had married in 1949 and their two children, Nicholas and Susan.

Charles Mitchel was born in Dublin in 1920 and went to a very good school, Clongowes Wood in County Kildare. From there, he went to Trinity College to study forestry, but became so engrossed in the Trinity Players that he never finished his degree. Instead, he immediately joined the Longford Players at the Gate Theatre. He went on to become a founding member of Irish Actors Equity and was also president of the Catholic Stage Guild.

When he joined the new television service, his first week's pay was £26, a small fortune in those days. His most memorable broadcast was a news flash the night that US President John F. Kennedy was assassinated, on 22 November 1963. Even though television in those days was black and white, Charles Mitchel appeared on screen ashen faced. He retired from RTÉ in 1984. Later, he had a brief spell as a presenter in 1989 with LMFM in Drogheda.

Keenly interested in animal welfare, he also bred basset hounds and was frequently seen taking them for walks in the Dundrum area. He died in the Bloomfield Nursing Home, Donnybrook, in 1996.

SARAH MITCHELL

The Mitchell family once had a splendid restaurant and bakery at number 10 Grafton Street in Dublin city centre, where a branch of McDonalds now stands. In the mid-nineteenth century, Mitchell's restaurant was run by Mrs Sarah Mitchell, who had excellent connections. She was a confectioner not only to the Lord Lieutenant of Ireland but to Queen Victoria. Yet despite being a busy woman, she lived some considerable distance from Dublin, in the then country district of Dundrum where, in the 1850s, she and her family only had about ten neighbours for company. The family were connected to Mitchell's, the present-day wine firm in Dublin.

DEREK MOONEY

One of the best-known and popular presenters on RTÉ radio and television, Derek Mooney was born in 1967. His father worked in the old VW assembly plant at Shelbourne Road in Ballsbridge. Derek's first job at RTÉ was in 1984, when he was a runner, working through the night on the station's coverage of the Los Angeles Olympics. He first made his name on radio, presenting wildlife programmes and he still does the all-night dawn chorus broadcast at the beginning of May every year. From 2001 until 2008 he presented the *Winning Streak* National Lottery show on television and continues to do much television work. His weekday afternoon radio show on Radio 1, running since 1995, continues to be very popular. Derek Mooney lives on Upper Kilmacud Road.

MULVEY FAMILY

The Mulveys have been noted personalities in the Dundrum area for well over eighty years. They came to Dundrum in 1928 from Rathmines, where they had a drapery shop on the site where Saunders' hardware shop once stood. The Mulveys opened a similar shop in Dundrum's Main Street. Next door to it was a shop belonging to Blanchardstown Mills, which had a chain of grocery shops across Dublin selling loose groceries. However, the Mulveys soon discovered a local demand for hardware and then builders' supplies, so the hardware shop developed. Within a few years, the drapery side of the business has been phased out and Mulveys builders' supplies became a familiar landmark. People used to say that if 'you couldn't get it in Mulveys, you couldn't get it anywhere.'

One of the earlier members of the family by marriage was P.V. Doyle, who became a famous hotelier. He built and opened what was the Burlington Hotel in 1972 and went on to found a noted chain of hotels in Dublin. His first hotel had been the Montrose Hotel on the Stillorgan Road in 1964, but is now a student hostel. P.V. Doyle died in 1988.

Another particularly well-known member of the family was Mary Mulvey, who was a local councillor for years and eventually became the chairman of Dublin County Council. In the 1960s she was also the chairman of the Meath Hospital in Dublin.

Six siblings make up the present generation of Mulveys – five boys and one girl. The original hardware shop premises was rebuilt in 1979 and is where Frank now runs Mulveys pharmacy, while Stephen is a GP whose practice is just across the street. The old hardware and builders' supply business was moved for a while by John to Ranelagh, but is now based in the Village Shopping Centre in Dundrum (the new name for the old shopping centre). The firm now concentrates on supplying wooden flooring.

CHRIS RYAN

The founder of the Ballinteer Family History Society in April 1993, Chris Ryan organised many events on the history of the area. He also wrote two books on the history of the church of St John the Evangelist in Ballinteer. The first was in 1998 for the twenty-fifth anniversary of the church and the second was for the thirtieth anniversary. He organised regular monthly meetings of the society in the conference room of the church and he was also instrumental in producing an annual journal every January called *Gateway to the Past*. When he moved to the midlands, the final lecture for the society took place in 2006. Chris died in January 2008 and was survived by his wife, Lily.

GEORGE JOHNSTONE STONEY

Born near Birr, County Offaly in 1826, he was the physicist responsible for introducing the concept of the electron, so essential in the modern digital age. From 1852 to 1857 he was Professor of Physics at Queen's College, Galway, now NUI Galway. In 1857 he took up a civil service job, as secretary of the Queen's University of Ireland. Despite giving up teaching, he continued his work of scientific exploration and was closely involved with the RDS, where he published seventy-five scientific research papers. He introduced the concept of electrons in 1881 and ten years later, invented the word 'electron'. Married to his cousin Margaret Sophie, they had two sons and three daughters. For many years they lived in Dundrum, and the road where they lived was renamed Stoney Road in his honour. After he retired in 1893, he and his family moved to London and he died at his home in Notting Hill in 1911. After cremation, his ashes were returned to Ireland and buried at St Nahi's.

FRANCIS STUART

A very controversial writer, Francis Stuart and his wife Madeleine, in their twilight years, lived in a bungalow in Windy Arbour. The terrace they lived in was adjacent to the Central Mental Hospital. Stuart had been born in Australia in 1902 to Protestant parents who came from the North of Ireland. When he was 18 he married Iseult, the daughter of Maud Gonne, a revolutionary leader. Stuart himself fought in the 1922-23 Civil War on the republican side, and was interned.

His first novel, *Women and God*, was published in 1931. Of his many novels, perhaps the most famous was *Black List Section H*, published in 1971 when Stuart was already a pensioner. During World War II he worked for the propaganda radio station beamed at Ireland by the Nazis and his period there, from 1942 to 1944, proved very controversial, dogging his later life.

After his wife Iseult died in 1954, he married Madeleine Meissner, whom he had met in Germany. After Madeleine died, he married for a third time, to an artist called Finola Graham, in 1987. Towards the end of his life, they moved to County Clare and Francis Stuart died on 2 February 2000. Just after he died, *The Irish Times* published a memorable colour photograph of the great writer lying on his death-bed.

Noted writer Dermot Bolger remembers that in the mid-1980s, he and his late wife always used to wheel their bicycles up the driveway of the Stuart house on the Sunday before Christmas. Francis sat there with a white cat in his lap. Once the dinner had been cooked, Francis opened the bottle of Chianti brought by the Bolgers to remind Madeleine of when they were starving, homeless refugees in the Germany of 1945. After dinner, in the twilight of the living room, she lit the German advent wreath she loved. Dermot Bolger also recalled that Madeleine's love of Francis was so great that they felt she would not outlast him long. In fact she died fourteen years before him. Dermot Bolger's last service to her, as her publisher, was to correct a misprint on her coffin.

DR ISAAC WILLIAM USHER

Isaac William Usher was a noted doctor in Dundrum, where he and his family lived for many years at Laurel Lodge. He was pre-deceased by his wife Rose in 1909. Dr Usher was the local dispensary doctor and most of his patients were local Catholic working-class residents of Dundrum. He also represented Dundrum on Rathdown District Council. Dr Usher died on 24 February 1917. He was always a bad timekeeper and he was rushing to get a train at Dundrum station when he was knocked down and killed by a car driven by another local resident, 'Batty' Hyland. Dr Usher was buried in the nearby St Nahi's graveyard.

He was much more controversial in death than in life. The local Church of Ireland community raised the funds to erect a memorial in his memory, but refused donations from local Catholics. That in itself created bad feeling, then during the 1920s, when the local Orange Order was still active, the 12 July route was from St Nahi's church to the Usher monument.

The monument has had various locations in the centre of Dundrum, but today it can be seen in the lower Main Street, beside the main entrance to the Luas station.

His eldest son, also called Isaac William, was killed in action during the First World War and is buried on the Somme.

JOHN L. WHITE

A respected local physician, John White died in 1870, aged 65, and is buried at St Nahi's. A monument was erected there by a few personal friends and some of the inhabitants of Dundrum, in remembrance of his many social qualities, his care and his kindness as a doctor and especially his attention to the poor of the village and surrounding district.

9

SCHOOLS

BALLINTEER INSTITUTE

Located at the Holy Cross School on the Upper Kilmacud Road, near the crossroads in Dundrum, it offers Leaving Certificate and Junior Certificate courses.

DUNDRUM COLLEGE OF FURTHER EDUCATION

Located on Main Street, the college has a wide selection of courses, in business studies, computer studies, design, health and community services and general studies. It offers both day and evening classes.

On the ground floor of the Carnegie Library in Dundrum, a prep school had been run between 1923 and 1938 by the Misses Carroll and Nesbit. At the same time, vocational school classes in Dundrum had their origins in the library.

The library remained in use for vocational teaching until the 1950s. The boys' technical college opened in 1957, then the new vocational school for girls opened in 1965. The last principal of Dundrum College was Brian Dornan, who retired in 2008 and who still lives in the Dundrum area. The present college, built within the last twenty years, is on the site of the old vocational school.

DUNDRUM GAELSCOIL

The new Irish-medium post-primary school, Gael-Choláiste an Phiarsaigh, is under the patronage of An Foras Pátrún. It's co-educational and multi-denominational.

EDUCATE TOGETHER, BALLINTEER

The Educate Together second-level school is due to open in Ballinteer in 2016, the results of local campaigning for such a school for over a decade. The pre-elementary school opened in 2010 and over 120 families pre-enrolled their children in the first three hours. In March, 2012 the Department of Education and Skills approved the national school in Ballinteer for Educate Together and it opened in May 2012, with Marie Gordon as principal.

HOLY CROSS NATIONAL SCHOOL

This long-established national school, on Upper Kilmacud Road, just opposite the Garda station in Dundrum, goes back well over two centuries. Many of its roll books have been kept and the oldest one in existence is dated 1801. It had become a national school when that system was instituted in 1831 and the site of the original school is now occupied by the extension to Holy Cross church. Access to the school was down a steep flight of steps from Ballinteer Road. In its earlier days, when the school was beside Holy Cross, accommodation was at a premium and the Carnegie Library had to be used as extra teaching accommodation. Even the old courthouse had to be pressed into service. In those far-off days, pupils usually had to walk to or from school as bus services were few and far between and it was almost unheard of for parents to own cars.

In the 1920s the school had babies who spent their days playing with plasticine and wooden bricks, while the older children, aged about six, more constructively learned the letters of the alphabet and numbers.

Beside the old school, at the rear of Holy Cross church, a small private school was run in the parlour of the house owned by Mr Coen, the father of one of the lady teachers at Holy Cross. The private school had a mere ten pupils, a fraction of the 200 or so during the 1920s in the national school.

According to the principal, Ultan MacMathúna, the original school on the present site was built in 1944, replacing old buildings by the Holy Cross Church. The site of the old school was in time used for the building of the extension to Holy Cross church in 1953. The site of the new school once consisted of open fields. But the new school saw a big improvement in facilities.

At the new school, the boys were upstairs and the girls downstairs. Numbers continued to expand rapidly as the district was developed. By the 1970s, pupils at the school numbered over 1,000. The present buildings were largely constructed in 1979, with further extensions made since then. The boys and girls schools were amalgamated in 1987. The school has had many outstanding teachers over the years and one of the most respected was Pearse Morris, principal of the boys school in the 1960s who was described by Jerry Cronin, a former CEO of County Dublin Vocational Educational Committee as being a 'mason, teacher, writer, philosopher and a man for all seasons'.

Among the past pupils of Holy Cross who have gone on to fame are Eamon Ryan, the leader of the Green Party; Nick Sweeney, a champion discus thrower in the 1990s; and Stephen Roche, the ace racing cyclist and winner of the Tour de France, who was born in Dundrum in 1958 and grew up in the district.

The number of pupils at the start of the 2014-15 school year was about 240, about half and half boys and girls. One of the distinguished members of the board of management is the local historian John G. Lennon.

The school has a very active sports programme as well as lots of drama. It has a science laboratory and a computer room, and as with schools generally, the old blackboards and chalk have been replaced by electronic whiteboards. Dundrum Montessori School is located at Holy Cross.

IRISH MANAGEMENT INSTITUTE

The institute was founded in 1952 and one of those involved in its foundation was Todd Andrews, then managing director of Bord na Mona and a long-time resident of Taney. Dr Liam Dillon Digby, managing director of the Pye factory in Dundrum, was also very involved.

It had a wandering existence, including a house on Orwell Road, Rathgar, which now houses the Russian embassy. Finally, in 1970, the Irish Management Institute found the ideal site, a nineteenth-century house called Clonard standing on just over 5 hectares off Sandyford Road.

The new centre was designed by Arthur Gibney & Partners in a very modernistic style, with its outer shell made entirely from concrete. The design was the Royal Institute of the Architects of Ireland's gold medal winner in 1974.

This building cost £1.2 million to construct and it was formally opened on 25 September 1974. One person closely involved with the institute was Diarmuid O'Broin, who was the advertisement manager of *Management* magazine. It had been launched as a proper magazine in 1967 and lasted until 1996. For much of that time, O'Broin, a colourful character who had previously worked in Eason's advertising agency, ran the commercial side of the magazine. He had a great sense of humour and often used to sign letters to potential advertisers 'O'Broin, the Baron of Barr-na-Coille'. After one of the revamps of the magazine, in 1982, he sent out a letter saying, 'we intend to make our competition look like tired old wastepaper'. He worked with several distinguished editors, whose ranks had included Dominick Coyle and Howard Kinlay. Diarmuid O'Broin died in Dublin in August, 2013.

Today, the Irish Management Institute has about fifty staff and about 3,000 professionals a year take its many management training courses, a total of about 200 a year. The institute also has a conference centre and residence on the site, retains the original Clonard House and has been in alliance with University College Cork since 2011.

MOUNT ANVILLE

In October 2013, the prestigious Montessori, primary and secondary schools at Mount Anville celebrated 160 years to the day since their founding on 18 October 1853. That was in Glasnevin, on Dublin's northside, when the first Dublin school opened.

In 1865, the school was transferred to Mount Anville and has been there ever since. The school was set up by the Sisters of the Sacred Heart, but in 2007 the running of the schools at Mount Anville was handed over to a trust, designed to preserve its educational ethos.

The Society of the Sacred Heart had been founded in Paris in 1800 by Sophie Borat. The order came to Ireland in 1842, starting up in Roscrea, County Tipperary. It opened in Armagh in 1851, and then came to Glasnevin in 1853.

Mount Anville had been bought from William Dargan, the previous owner and occupier of the house, in 1865 and a photograph taken the following year shows pupils in front of the building. The tower at Mount Anville, built by Dargan, can be clearly seen in the background. For many years after the school had arrived at Mount Anville, the farm was very important in providing food for the school and the convent as well as for the locality. From the 1950s the order started to sell off the farmland, which was used for housing developments, but the original greenhouses are still in place.

However, despite popular preconceptions, Mount Anville isn't the most expensive secondary school in Ireland. It's less expensive than Alexandra College in Milltown and St Andrew's College in Booterstown, which caters for boys and girls. Holy Child in Killiney is a religious girls school and it too is more expensive than Mount Anville.

On the day of the celebrations in 2013, the conference was addressed by a past pupil, Catherine Day, secretary general of the European Commission, while another old girl, TV presenter Sybil Mulcahy, was the Mistress of Ceremonies for the day. The long list of past pupils present included Alison Doody, the actress; TV presenter Lisa Cannon; hockey player Emma Gray and Myra Garrett, managing partner of William Fry, a leading Dublin firm of solicitors.

NOTRE DAME

The Notre Dame School was founded in 1953 by the Notre Dame des Missions Sisters, who withdrew from education in Ireland in 2002. The school is now run by a charitable trust. It's a fee paying Catholic girls secondary school and there's also a junior school and a Montessori school. The chairman of the school trust is well-known businessman Mark Mortell.

OUR LADY'S GROVE, GOATSTOWN

The original school was founded in 1963 and on its first day, there were thirty-three pupils, of whom fifteen were ready for their first year of secondary school. Secondary school recognition came in February 1964. Alongside the secondary school, the Jesus and Mary Primary School has flourished as well over the past fifty years.

The school started as a private school, but in 1971 it became a public national school. On 25 June 2013 the Catholic Archbishop of Dublin, Diarmuid Martin, officiated at the blessing and opening of the new school. In 2014 the fiftieth anniversary of the primary school was extensively celebrated. That year also saw the new school library being equipped.

The order that founded the school, the Sisters of Jesus and Mary, was started by a French nun called Sister Claudine who had managed to escape the French Revolution after her brothers had been executed. She founded an order with a philosophy based on love and forgiving enemies. The Sisters of Jesus and Mary had opened their first house in Ireland at Sandford Road Ranelagh in 1955.

OUR LADY'S GIRLS NATIONAL SCHOOL, BALLINTEER AVENUE

This national school shares a campus with Our Lady's Boys School and pre-school facilities. It's close to Marlay Park and to St John the Evangelist church and the St Michael's House facility.

QUEEN OF ANGELS PRIMARY SCHOOL, WEDGEWOOD

This school opened in 1981 under the patronage of the Catholic Archbishop of Dublin, to cater for the growth in the number of schoolgoing children at primary level in the Balally and Sandyford areas.

ST OLAF'S NATIONAL SCHOOL, BALALLY DRIVE

In 2014, this was one of the national schools throughout the country that had remedial work done on its structures, after several years when financial constraints meant this work couldn't be done. It caters for both boys and girls. Originally, there were two schools on the site, Balally Boys School and Balally Girls School. Mrs Brigid Cannon was the first principal of the latter school, while Frank Kelleher was the first principal of the boys' school. The girls' school became St Olaf's in 1974 and as the parish was expanding very rapidly, there was an evident need for a brand new school, as the existing two schools were very overcrowded, while the playgrounds were filled with prefabs.

So the Queen of Angels Primary School was opened in 1981 and St Olaf's, which had been founded in 1968 and which is named after Olaf the White, the Viking who became the first king of Viking Dublin, took over the former boys' school building. As for Olaf, he was reputed to have built a fort in the Balally area and indeed, Balally derives its name from the Irish for 'town of Olaf'.

A new extension was built to St Olaf's in 2011 and resources at the school now include sixteen mainstream classrooms, nine resource rooms, a new library and a state-of-the-art computer room.

TANEY NATIONAL SCHOOL

This Church of Ireland primary school is the largest such school in the Republic. Its origins in the Dundrum area go back to the eighteenth century. The earliest records show that it was established as a parochial school for the underprivileged in the parish in 1792, but it's thought that a school had existed in Taney before then. The first recorded schoolmaster at Taney was Henry Curran, appointed in May 1790 by the Archbishop of Dublin. One of the earliest schoolmistresses was rather sadly made redundant because of her advancing age.

Children didn't just receive lessons, but food and clothes as well. For the year 1793, £15 was spent on food for the pupils, equivalent to about €500 in today's money. In 1859, a new parochial school house, together with a residence for the schoolmaster, was built at Eglinton Terrace by Lord Pembroke.

The charitable status lasted until 1898, when the school joined the national school system. The first principal teacher under the national school system was Joseph McCaughey, who came from Strangford, County Down (1898 to 1928). His wife Mary also taught in the school, until 1938. All the pupils at the school were Protestant up until 1904 when the first two Catholic pupils, John Richard Scanlon and Percy Scanlon, signed up.

But the number of Catholic children at the school remained tiny until the 1970s. Up until the 1960s, the school was serving a relatively rural community and pupil numbers only increased by a third between 1920 and 1960. But during the 1960s, with the start of so many housing developments in the area, rapid expansion of pupil numbers started. The old school buildings soon proved inadequate and a site for a new school was found at Sydenham Villas. The new school was designed by the Office of Public Works. Originally it was a six-teacher school but even as it was being built, it was being extended.

The new school was opened by the then Minister for Education, Pádraig Faulkner, on Saturday, 21 November 1970. The new school cost £45,000 to build of which the local contribution was 25 per cent.

By nine years later in 1979, the school had expanded so much that it had eighteen teachers. Bobby Smyth was a very energetic principal from 1959 until his retirement in 1978, when he was succeeded by the equally dynamic Beryl Tilson, the first female principal in the school's history. She retired in 2000. Since then, a substantial new building programme has been carried out at the school, which has close to 500 pupils, with over thirty full-time teachers and around fifteen more part-time teachers.

WESLEY COLLEGE, BALLINTEER

This renowned college dates back to 1845, when a Wesleyan school was opened at St Stephen's Green, Dublin. For many years, the college was closely associated with St Stephen's Green, but by the 1920s it had started expanding in the Upper Leeson Street area.

In 1948, Burlington House was purchased in that immediate area, while the next door Burleigh House was bought twelve years later. Eventually, the college outgrew its four sites in the Upper Leeson Street area and what was the Burlington Hotel was subsequently built on part of those sites.

In 1964, the college paid £55,000 for Ludford Farm on Ballinteer Road and eventually a brand new college was built on the site. School activities on the old site in Ballinteer ended in June 1969, the new buildings at Ludford Park having been dedicated the previous week. The original Ludford House, with its walled gardens, became the headmaster's house. Today, Wesley College remains a noted co-educational day and boarding school.

10

SHOPPING

JOE DALY'S CYCLE SHOP

Joe Daly opened his first cycle shop in Dundrum in October 1951. It remained in place until 1973, when the second shop was opened, on the site of the current outlet. It remained there until 2001, when it was moved to Main Street. The shop moved again in November 2006, when it reached its present venue, the 'round tower' beside the Dargan Luas bridge.

The shop is one of the oldest established cycle shops in the country and David Tansey, now the owner and a son of the late Joe Daly, remembers that in the old days, new bicycles would be left outside all day. Also in the old days, the shop used to do electrical repairs, as well as selling electrical goods and the likes of oil-fired heaters. These days, Joe Daly's Cycle shop has gone back to its original roots and is strictly a cycle shop, for commuting cyclists and serious sporting cyclists alike.

DUNDRUM POST OFFICE

This local post office is now located on Main Street, close to the crossroads. Situated in various locations over the years, Dundrum has had a post office on its main street since 1810, when the first one opened.

DUNDRUM SHOPPING CENTRE

This opened in 1971 and was considered to have been the second such centre to open in Ireland. The country's first shopping centre opened at nearby Stillorgan in 1966. The Dundrum centre was built on the Glenville farmlands on the western side of Main Street. The shopping centre was badly designed, in an L shape, while the car park was too small, meaning that people had to walk a distance from the larger car park at the northern end of the complex. The centre had Five Star (then Quinnsworth, which in turn became Tesco) as its anchor tenant. The original shopping centre was noted for the Bewley's café on the upper floor, as well as the record shop, also on the upper level.

This Tesco branch moved to the Dundrum Town Centre and the supermarket was acquired by Lidl, who are still there today in the renamed Dundrum Village Centre. Another tenant is Dealz, which sells all its products at fixed low prices, while round at the back of the centre is a big electrical and electronic retailer, Dominic Smith.

After the Dundrum Town Centre was built, the plan was for the old shopping centre to be demolished and rebuilt as phase two of the town centre, but this never happened. Instead, the old shopping centre carries on, and is now renamed as the Dundrum Village Centre.

DUNDRUM TOWN CENTRE

This is now by far the biggest employer in the area, with about 5,500 people working for shops, leisure facilities and other companies within the centre. Work on the centre had begun in 1999 on what had been the Pye lands. It was built by Joe O'Reilly and when it opened, on 3 March 2005, it had a staggering 112,000 square metres of shopping and leisure space. Altogether, it has over 135 retail outlets.

The first day it opened, the centre, which had cost €850 million to build, attracted 75,000 visitors keen to see what new delights it offered. It gets about 20 million visitors a year, who spend more here than in any other Irish shopping centre. Dundrum Town Centre is the largest such centre in Ireland and, under centre director Don Nugent, it has won a plethora of awards for excellence, including European Shopping Centre of the Year.

Many international retailers have set up shop in the centre, including Harvey Nichols, House of Fraser, Marks & Spencer and Tesco. While many of the international chains, including Marks & Spencer and Tesco have numerous other branches in Ireland, for others, such as Harvey Nichols and House of Fraser, the Dundrum Town Centre is their only presence in this part of Ireland.

A whole range of international fashion retailers, in addition to the aforementioned, also operate in the centre, such as Monsoon, River Island and Zara. Other specialised retailers, like Boots and HMV,

also have outlets. Overall, it means that customers have an incredible choice of fashion, beauty and footwear, accessories, giftware, homeware, in fact, everything for the person and the home.

One of the big retail openings in the centre came in October 2008 when Hamleys, noted for its Regent Street London toy store, opened its first European standalone store. It occupies 3,500 square metres on three floors in the Pembroke district of the centre. The shop has a vast range of toys that appeal to all ages, including more traditional and nostalgic toys. Another big opening came in 2011, when the first Irish Hollister fashion store opened its doors. According to Hollister's parent company, Abercrombie & Fitch, this new Hollister store greatly exceeded expectations.

The Big Bang bookshop is one of the most intriguing smaller shops. It specialises in the best of new comics, as well as out of print rarities and it has a big range of comic book merchandise and memorabilia.

A really popular shopping event is the Shop and Rock, which happens twice a year, once in either the spring or summer, then again during the autumn or winter. These fun-filled nights of music and discounts begin at 7 p.m. and continue until midnight, attracting huge customer support.

One feature for shoppers is the Shopmobility scheme, which lends manual wheelchairs, powered wheelchairs and mobility scooters to members of the public who have limited mobility, enabling them to enjoy the leisure and commercial opportunities in the centre. There is a substantial number of car parking spaces underneath, 3,400 in all, as well as an adjoining Tesco filling station.

Shoppers can also avail of the personal style team service. The stylists know the offerings of the centre's retailers inside out and if someone signs up for a one-to-one session with a stylist, it lasts two hours and costs €65. The team is described as 'a shoppers-go-to-team, trusted advisers and most honest friend all rolled into one'. Shoppers can also use the Dundrum e-giftcard scheme, a pre-loaded debit card that can be redeemed at over 150 outlets throughout the centre.

Dundrum Town Centre also uses social media platforms, Twitter, Facebook and Instagram to interact with the public. These accounts are managed by the centre's marketing team. The Facebook page has well over 100,000 likes and through Facebook, the 'Dundrum Delights' app has competitions and giveaways. Altogether, all these social media platforms are used to communicate key messages and engage with the centre's customers.

There's also a Dundrum mobile app on iPhone and Android and it is updated in real time with the Dundrum Town Centre website, but all the images and text are specific to mobile users.

FINDLATER'S

Findlater's was one of the splendid old-time shops in Dundrum that has long since disappeared, along with a similar establishment, Leverett & Frye. Findlater's shops were once an institution in the Dublin area and at the company's AGM in 1945, it was announced that in the year under review, the new Findlater's shop had been started at 14 Main Street in Dundrum, managed by Robert Campbell. Findlater's offered an old fashioned over-the-counter grocery service, as well as an excellent selection of wines. The chain of shops joined in the supermarket revolution, which was just starting in Ireland in the late 1960s, but failed to compete with the new-look supermarkets, run by the likes of H. Williams, which also operated in Dundrum. Findlater's shop in Dundrum closed down in 1969 along with the rest of the chain.

HEALTHWAVE SHOP

This unique pharmacy started in the Dundrum Town Centre in December 2013, and already it has been a big hit with customers all over the country. It was the idea of Shane O'Sullivan, who graduated from UCC in 2009. The plan with his new shop is to sell mostly generic drugs at cut-price margins so that the retail price of those drugs is on a par with what's available in Northern Ireland.

Customers pay a small annual fee to join the 'club' and they can then get these low-price drugs, which are delivered all over the country, an absolute boon for people who are on long-term heavy medication.

HUMAN APPEAL IRELAND

The unique charity shop opened in 2014, part of a new chain of charity shops in Dublin. In Dundrum, the shop is located in the old Apollo Building on Dundrum Road, beside the Dargan Luas bridge. The shop sells all kinds of craft items, handmade by Syrian refugees who have set up micro-businesses of their own in the countless refugees camps bordering Syria that have been created since the civil war in Syria began in 2011. As for Human Appeal, the charity behind this latest Dundrum charity shop, it began life in a one-bedroomed flat in Manchester in 1991 and is now operational in around twenty-five countries across three continents. Other longer established charity shops in Dundrum are Women's Aid and Oxfam, both on Main Street.

Drink and Enjoy OUR   **Our Excelsior Blend**

Celebrated **TEAS**   A SPECIALITY.   **2/-**
1/6 to 2/6 per lb.

2d. per lb. Discount for Parcels of 5 lbs. and upwards

LEVERETT & FRYE, LTD.,
Main Street, DUNDRUM.

LEVERETT & FRYE

Once one of the main grocery shops on Dundrum's Main Street, Leverett & Frye had been established there long before the arrival of Findlater's and in the mid-1930s, was still going strong. What was the Leverett & Frye shop building had been constructed by local builder John Richardson, as indicated by a plaque that says it was constructed in 1881.

The shop had opened in 1896 and it held an agency for W&A Gilbey, the wine people. In the days before supermarket self-service shopping had been developed, customers placed their orders with assistants at the counter. Many of the customers were people who worked as servants for the aristocrats who then lived in the district. Shopping was a much more leisurely affair in those days and the people coming into the shop usually had plenty of time for a chat with the shop assistants.

However, around a century ago, shopping in Dundrum's Main Street had its drawbacks. The road wasn't properly paved, so that in summer, clouds of dust flew up whenever vehicles went past. In winter, on the other hand, the street had many puddles and mud. In those far off days, the infrequent traffic in Main Street consisted of horse-drawn carts delivering to the shops, including milk carts with churns of milk, and the occasional horse-drawn omnibus.

When customers went into Leverett & Frye, they were assailed by a variety of delicious smells, including freshly ground coffee, fresh bread and smoked bacon. Loose tea was weighed out from bins, while butter was cut from huge blocks, which never went off, despite the complete lack of refrigeration. The shop had twelve open tins of biscuits, so that customers could mix and match as they pleased.

Two of the staff in the Dundrum shop, well known in the earlier 1960s, were Sean and Tommy Cronin. Leverett & Frye closed down in the late 1960s and in 1968, they bought the old Leverett & Frye shop in

Rathgar and turned it into the Gourmet Shop. Leverett & Frye's former shop at the crossroads in Dundrum became Ladbroke's bookmakers.

MOSS COTTAGE

Number 4 Pembroke Cottages on Dundrum's Main Street once housed the town's Social Welfare offices, but today, it has something entirely different, Moss Cottage, run by Jen Cleary.

She studied design and sculpture at the National College of Art and Design in Dublin and is an expert on home crafts. Jen was the manager of the gift shop at Airfield until she was made redundant in 2011, so she then started Moss Cottage as a unique gift shop, quirky and eclectic. Apart from lots of very unusual gift items, she also stocks vintage and kitsch items.

The shop has lots of unique presents that cost less than €10, while she also puts together wedding hampers. Jen also does classes in wedding planning and it's all helped by the fact that Moss Cottage has a strong social media presence.

When *The Irish Times* did a feature on the shop in 2013, reader reaction was enthusiastic, with some saying that Moss Cottage was friendly and welcoming, a gem of a find, while others commented that the attention to detail was second to none.

OLD SHOPS

In the old days Dundrum's Main Street had a plethora of small shops, each more eccentric than the next. Dundrum then had seven terraces in and around Main Street and, surprisingly, nearly all of them still survive today, even though the small shops they housed are long gone.

Close by Waldemar Terrace, next to the library, was a row of nine cottages and a small huckster's shop owned by the Tobin family. It had a great variety of goods and was as much a hardware store as a grocery shop, but it and all the cottages are long since gone. Brennan's shop on Main Street, which was a newsagency and general shop, was the first shop in the area to have its own electricity, supplied by a generator in the back garden. The man who owned this shop also had a tea importing business and he started tea rooms on the first floor above the shop. But in those days the population of Dundrum was too slight to support such a venture.

Next to Brennan's was a taxi business and a Shell petrol pump run by Peter Byrne, with only one grade of petrol on offer. The entrance

MAIN STREET,
And BALINTEER ROAD.

Dundrum, _____ July 18 _____ 1925

M.rs. J. Nolan

Bought of **J. CLANCY,**

Grocery, Wine and Spirit Merchant. £ 6 19

June			£ s d
11	2 loaves 10½	1lb Onions 3	1 1½
13	2 loaves 10½	1½ polish 2	1 0½
16	4 heads Cabbage 6	1 coal 5½	11¼
18	3	1lb 1 fice	8½
19	2 loaves 10	½ Rashrs 4 10	1 Onions 3	2 11½
	1lb 1 Butter		1 8
20	L.K. Sand 1½	Soap 3½	1 1
21	2 loaves		10½
23	polish 2	½ lbs flour 5d	7
25	1 lb Rashrs 10	26 2 loaves 10½	1lb Onions 3	2 1½
26	½ st flour		1 4½
28	bag 5½	½ lb Cheese 9	1 2¼
29	½ lb 1 Rashrs		11
30	½ st Potatoes 6	2 heads Cabbage 5	11
	1 lb 1 Rashrs 11	½ st Potatoes 3	1 2
	1lb Onions 3	Salt 6	9
	Forward		£1 0 3

CAMPBELL,

CAMPBELL'S CORNER Bootmaker

CORNER DUNDRUM

REPAIRS TURNED OUT EQUAL TO NEW BY RECENTLY |
INSTALLED UP-TO-DATE FINISHING MACHINERY. |

| HAND-SEWN REPAIRS. | NO JOB TOO CRITICAL. |
| SOLUTION PATCHES. | NO JOB TOO SMALL. |

to the garage had many occupiers, including a grocery shop, a pork butcher, and in more recent times, a TV rental shop and then a retail outlet for jeans, QT One. Yet another shop on Main Street was a drapery shop run first by Mrs Byrne and then by a man called T.J. Ringrose, who was the father of Col Billy Ringrose, the famous army equestrian rider. Among his subsequent achievements was as President of the Royal Dublin Society (RDS).

A shop with no window was well-known to Dundrum residents, housing George Kinahan's gents' hairdresser for over forty years. These days the mens' barber shop on Main Street is tucked underneath the stairs in the Dundrum Village Centre.

The Bargain King on Main Street was originally Murphys newsagents, tobacconists and confectioners. Murphys also became the starting point for city-bound buses. But its successor, Bargain King, was very popular with children, since it had the first 'one armed bandit' in Dundrum. These days, all the old style shops along Main Street in Dundrum have long since vanished, with one exception, Campbell's Corner, where Paul Campbell still does shoe repairs, at the crossroads, at the corner of Main Street and Ballinteer Road.

Before the Dundrum Shopping Centre (1971) now called the Dundrum Village Centre, there was a big house called Glenville, which had a number of occupiers over the years, including a man called Riordan, a one-time Crown solicitor.

SUPERMARKET WARS

Just past where the Dundrum Town centre is located, close to the present-day Wyckham Way, Dundrum once had a thriving supermarket venue, which lasted from the mid-1960s until construction started on the Dundrum Town Centre. The original supermarket had been built as an extension to the Pye factory. At one stage, there was even a factory here for the Hafner sausage firm.

In the early 1970s an entrepreneur called Albert Gubay started a chain of discount stores at various locations, including Dundrum. They were called Three Guys. Then in 1978, Tesco bought Three Guys and relaunched the supermarkets, but the venture wasn't a success. Tesco eventually pulled out of the Irish market and did not return until 1997, when it took over Quinnsworth from Associated British Foods.

When it left the Irish market in 1986, Tesco sold the discount chain to H. Williams, which in turn collapsed the following year during a price war. Dundrum became known for Super Crazy Prices, an early Tesco offering, where merchandise was piled on pallets at discount prices. Crazy Prices was one of the first supermarkets to start late-night shopping, opening until 9 p.m. When the Dundrum Shopping Centre opened, a long vanished supermarket chain called Five Star, run by D.E. Williams of Tullamore Dew fame, set up shop there, but this was later taken over by Quinnsworth, in turn taken over by Tesco and now by Lidl.

Jacaveline Holohan

The area also has a much smaller shopping centre, the Balally shopping centre on Blackthorn Avenue in Sandyford.

ROSEMOUNT SHOPS

Rosemount, that part of Dundrum Road between Windy Arbour and the Dargan Luas bridge, was a poor working-class district eighty years ago. It had lots of small cottages where conditions were so bad that, in one case, a group of fifty cottages had one small outdoor lavatory. Those ancient dwellings have long since been swept away or modernised, while the small shops that characterised Rosemount have also vanished. They included O'Connors butcher's, Hayes and Hayes chemist's and Byrne's grocery. Just about the only retail establishment left from the old days is Uncle Tom's Cabin, although it has long since surrendered its grocery shop. One old time shop in Rosemount called Hadnett's seemed to sell just about everything. So if a customer wanted half a dozen tomatoes, a packet of Sweet Afton cigarettes or a spool of thread, this shop had it.

11

SPORT

CYCLING

One of Ireland's best-known cyclists, Stephen Roche, comes from Dundrum, where he was born on 28 November 1959. His parents had lived in Ranelagh, but after they got married they moved to Dundrum, where the young lad turned out to be a star pupil at the Holy Cross National School. Roche began his working life as a mechanic in a dairy company, all the whole honing his cycling skills. He has long since left Dundrum, living in France since 1980. His big breakthrough came in 1987, when he won the Tour de France, the only Irish cyclist to have achieved this honour. The presentation at the end of the race, on the Champs-Elysées in Paris, has been long remembered because the then Taoiseach, Charles Haughey, made a special trip to Paris to greet Roche on the winner's podium and bask in his glory.

Stephen Roche is still very involved in cycling and cycle training and runs his holiday complex in Mallorca in Spain, where cyclists can go to boost their training in the Mediterranean sunshine. He set up this cycling holiday and training camp back in 1994.

Roche lives in Antibes in the south of France, where he owns and runs a hotel. In his spare time he is very involved in charity work and cycle challenges. Roche's commitment to cycling is reflected in the local cycling club, the Dundrum Town Centre Orwell Wheelers, the club with which Roche started cycling. It is closely involved in one of Ireland's main annual cycling events, the Stephen Roche Grand Prix. This is held on the 1.3 kilometres circuit in the housing estate at Ballinteer where no less than three of the Roche family took their first tentative pedal strokes. Roche's son Nicholas is now a leading cyclist. Nicholas, who was born in 1984, now lives in Italy and turned professional in 2004.

Following Roche's win in the Tour de France, a monument to him was erected in Main Street, Dundrum. Subsequently it was transferred to the Dundrum Town Centre, where it can now be seen beside the mill pond.

Dundrum has long had a reputation as a cycling hub, ever since Joe Daly started his first cycle shop there in the autumn of 1951. That first shop was beside the present-day traffic junction in Dundrum. Joe Daly was helped in fitting out the shop by a well-known footballer of the time, Ossie Nash. That first shop lasted until 1973, then the second shop was opened, also close by the junction. It was then moved, in 2001, to Main Street, Dundrum. The present cycle shop, its fourth location, is in a distinctive tower-like building beside the road junction and the Dargan Luas bridge. It was opened on 28 November 2006, which coincidentally was Stephen Roche's birthday.

JOE DALY

The name of Joe Daly Cycles has been inextricably linked with cycling in Dundrum and indeed much further afield, for over sixty years. Joe was born in Holles Street maternity hospital and brought up in

Dundrum by his aunt Ellen Daly. He later recalled that while he was a Tansey, he had taken his aunt's name. He lived on Ballinteer Road, across from the old Dundrum school, in a time when the landscape was largely rural. Joe served his time in Mellon's garage on Main Street, doing everything, including driving a taxi, looking after the bicycle section and doing bicycle repairs. While he was there, he went to Ringsend Technical School three nights a week for five years, learning everything he could about mechanical engineering, welding, electrical work and running a workshop.

The inevitable outcome was that Joe opened his first cycle shop in Dundrum. The first penny that Joe took in was from Mr Gleeson, who lived in Balally, who bought a valve rubber. While Joe was into cycles and motorbikes, he was also into many other non-sporting activities. He used to run dances up by Simpson's Hospital, and it was at one of those dances he met Kathleen, who became his wife. They and their family of three boys and three girls lived at nearby Westbrook Road. Today the cycle shop business is run by one of Joe's sons, David.

Joe remembered that in the 1950s, Hercules and Raleigh were the most popular bike brands, either single speed or basic three-speed models. He also recalled that in the 1950s a lot of women in the area were cyclists, but years later they all wanted cars.

In the mid-1950s, when people were becoming a bit better off, they gravitated towards auto bikes. Bicycles became popular again in the 1960s, and then in the 1980s, Dundrum-born cyclist Stephen Roche was one of the big names in cycling who helped make the sport and pastime popular again. Joe Daly always remained passionate about improving conditions for cyclists, including more cycle lanes. Up to the end of his life, Joe always cycled to and from his shop, a great believer in keeping fit. Joe was also passionately interested in community affairs and served as Mayor of Dundrum. Joe Daly died in February 2010.

DUNDRUM FOOTBALL CLUB

Dundrum Football Club plays its home games at the Meadow Wood Leisure Centre and has a senior team that plays in the Leinster Senior League non-intermediate division three. The under-age teams play in the Dublin and District Schoolboys' League and the South Dublin Football League. The club also field a women's senior team and an U18 girls' team. The 2013-14 season marked the club's fortieth anniversary.

DUNDRUM SOUTH DUBLIN ATHLETIC CLUB

Dundrum South Dublin Athletic Club is one of the leading athletic clubs in the country, with members of all levels and ages competing in track and field events, as well as in cross-country and road races. It had spent an exhausting twenty years looking for a location for a new clubhouse and the quest came to an end in 2013 when it paid €1.5 million at auction for St Thomas's House in Whitechurch, on the edge of Marlay Park, an old Georgian house on 6 hectares of land.

Originally, according to the club chairman Jim Kidd, they had been looking for land where they could build both a clubhouse and a track. However, the local council built a track at Marlay Park, which became the heart of the club. As St Thomas's House was situated only 400 metres from the park it seemed an ideal location for a clubhouse. It also had the added bonus of the nearby Dublin Mountains for those people who wanted to do longer runs and among the plans announced by the club following the purchase was a cross-country trail around the perimeter of the grounds.

At the time of the purchase Kidd stated: 'We're a community-based club in south Dublin ... This came on the market and it suited our needs perfectly. It was close to Marlay Park, the heart of our club, and suited our every need. We can hold seminars, meetings, small socials and more importantly, the younger members can have a safe environment to train and run in.'

Kidd was wary of not disrupting the idyllic setting too much: 'There's loads of potential. We wanted to be close to where the heart of our club is and despite the fact that we compete at Olympic level, we are very much a community-based club'.

The club has about 1,000 members at all levels, aged from 9 to 90. They compete from juniors right up to masters, while athletes take part in national and international events. The club was started in 1973 by Eddie and Liz McDonagh, as the Dundrum Family Recreation Centre Athletic Club. Some fifteen years later, the name was changed to the Dundrum and South Dublin Athletic Club, following the merger with the South Dublin Athletic Club. The new name reflects the wide geographical area from which its membership is drawn.

In its early years, stars included Carol Meagan, Carey May, Dave Taylor, Derek O'Connor, Olympians Nick Sweeney (discus), Victor Costello (shot) and Aisling Molloy (800 and 1,500 metres). In recent times, the club's most famous track and field athlete has been David Gillick, a double world champion and Olympian. He followed in the footsteps of a fellow athlete from the club, Robert Daly, also an Olympian.

DUNDRUM TABLE TENNIS CLUB

This club is the successor to Ballinteer Rangers ACF, which had been founded in 1933. The first meeting for the new club was in Val Dillon's shop in Rosemount and the club was formally opened in the 1970s by the then Taoiseach, Liam Cosgrave. The original clubhouse was a small portable hut at the entrance to Balally Park. In its most recent move, in May 2014, the club migrated to the sports hall in Benildus College on Upper Kilmacud Road, close to the Kilmacud station on the Luas Green Line. The club is now the largest of its kind in the Dublin area.

NAOMH OLAF GAA CLUB

When the area between Dundrum and Sandyford was developed in the late 1960s and early 1970s, a new parish was created, Balally, named after the largest of the new housing estates in the area. Mick Brown, who lived in Balally, had previously given years of outstanding service to the Naomh Fionbarra GAA club in Cabra and he was instrumental in starting up this new club. In July 1981, he called a meeting of ten interested residents and so the new club began. One of the schools in Balally had already been called St Olaf's, because the area derived its name from the son of Olaf, the Norse king of Dublin, the founder of Christchurch Cathedral in Dublin. The new club took the name of Olaf and adopted claret and blue as its colours.

In its first season, 1981-2, the club entered four football teams and two hurling teams and all the players were aged between 10 and 14. Over the years, many primary teachers in the area have contributed much to the club, including Gerry Murphy, Tom and Mick Brennan, Finbar O'Driscoll, Barry Kenna and Seamus O'Neill. The formation of the new club was widely welcomed in the whole area. Teachers in both schools in Ballaly Parish coached and encouraged the children to play Gaelic games. The club presented jerseys to the school teams and an excellent relationship developed between the schools and the club. The opening of the new clubhouse in April 1994 by the then president of the GAA, Jack Boothman, was a major milestone.

Situated adjacent to the playing fields at Wedgewood, it is spacious and well designed, with four dressing rooms equipped with showers, as well as a large sports hall and a lounge bar. In 2002, the club added to its building by getting an extension to the bar constructed. The extension also includes a fully fitted restaurant and kitchen, which means that the club can cater for large functions.

In 2012, a state-of-the-art hurling wall was built at the back of the clubhouse. In late 2003, the club held a special ceremony to rename the playing fields at Wedgewood, Pairc Bhriain. They were called after Barry O'Brien, who had died in tragic circumstances a year earlier. Barry had captained the Dublin U21 hurlers the summer before he died and he was also a very important player on the club's adult hurling team at midfield. Barry did much for the club in his short life and the club felt that naming the playing fields after him was the least that could be done to honour a remarkable young man.

DUNDRUM STEEPLECHASING

In the earlier nineteenth century, when Dundrum was still a country village, the locality was often used for steeplechasing. In December 1838, for instance, twenty horses took part in a steeplechase. Cricket, too, was a popular sport in Dundrum in the old days and in June 1960 the Manor team played the Airfield team, in the grounds of Airfield House.

MILLTOWN GOLF CLUB

This renowned golf club, the only one in the Dundrum area, dates back over a century. Its main entrance is at Lower Churchtown Road, just past Classon's bridge.

The foundations of the club date back to the autumn of 1906, when four devotees of the royal and ancient game met in the old Leinster Club, then located at 29 Leinster Street. Earlier that afternoon, when they had played eighteen holes at Portmarnock, they met at the Leinster Club and struck up a conversation over a game of snooker. The four men, John H. Callan, John Carberry, Frederick E. Davies and W.C. Pickeman, all from Dublin's southside, decided, just like that, to acquire land and build a golf course on their side of the city. As a result of that afternoon's conversation, the Milltown Golf Club was created.

Land was leased off the Lower Churchtown Road and on the banks of the River Dodder, sufficient for nine holes. The layout of the course was designed by F.E. Davies and W.C. Pickeman. A clubhouse was designed by architect G.L. O'Connor. Building work started in January 1907 and nine months later, on 29 September 1907, the first captain, F.E. Davies, drove the first ball to mark the opening of the club. The first president of the club was William Martin Murphy. Murphy lived in nearby Dartry and owned the *Irish Independent*, the *Evening Herald*, Clerys department store, the Dublin United Tramways Company and much else besides. He was the notorious head of the employers in the 1913 Dublin Lockout.

The year after the club opened, the first lady captain, Mrs Rose Byrne, was elected and James Martin was appointed the first professional at the club. In 1912, additional land was leased to extend the course to eighteen holes. The clubhouse was also extended to cater for both men and women. The layout of the new holes was also designed by F.E. Davies and W.C. Pickeman.

Then just over twenty years later, the first and second leases were bought out, in 1933 and 1934 respectively. The clubhouse acquired further extensions in 1923, the year that Milltown hosted the Irish Close Championship. In 1929, the Milltown Open Mixed Foursomes was inaugurated and this was recognised as the Irish Open Mixed Foursomes, attracting huge galleries of spectators as men and lady internationals competed. In the 1950s and 1960s, Joe Carr was the leading international in Ireland and England and he played in these foursomes with his first wife Dor, winning six times. These foursomes were then the biggest social event in golf and they lasted until 1994.

In the silver jubilee year of 1932, Dr Frank O'Grady was the captain, alongside Gen Nugent, the lady captain. They were invited to be the club captains again in the club's golden jubilee year of 1957. Professionals at the club during its long history have included James Martin, Tom Shannon, who was a wonderful teacher, Christy Greene, a legendary golfer, and in recent times, John Harnett, also a great teacher.

Greens, fairways and tees have all been redeveloped in recent years and Milltown is now considered one of the finest parkland courses in Ireland. The course has some fine views of the Dublin Mountains, especially from the fifth and eleventh holes.

Probably the most dramatic event in the club's history was the fire that destroyed the clubhouse on 5 September 1958. The clubhouse was completely burned out, along with 300 sets of clubs, but all the medals and trophies were saved. Thorncliffe House, adjacent to the second tee, became the club's temporary home until the new clubhouse was built. It was officially opened on 13 July 1960 and substantially refurbished in 2005. The course, too, has undergone development of its greens, fairways and tees, begun in 2006 and completed in 2008.

Members of Milltown Golf Club, besides distinguishing themselves in golf, have also won many distinctions in other sports, such as cricket, fencing, rugby and tennis. In 2007, the club celebrated its centenary in due style, including the publication of a fine illustrated centenary history.

12

TRANSPORT

BUILDING THE LUAS LINE

The Green Luas line from St Stephen's Green to Bride's Glen follows the route of the old Harcourt Street railway line from Dublin to Bray. Just beyond Dundrum, a special challenge faced the construction teams. At that point, the line goes through a deep cutting, an outlying spur of the Dublin Mountains, and during 2002 and 2003, much rock had to be removed to stabilise the sides of the cutting. Work is ongoing in Dublin city centre to connect the Green and Red lines. When is due for completion in 2015 and will make it much easier for passengers travelling from the Dundrum area to go into the city centre. When the cutting beyond Dundrum was being stabilised, it was also widened to allow for the planned new Metro system, but this has now been postponed indefinitely and it's not clear whether this planned new system will ever now come to fruition.

LUAS STATIONS

The old railway station at Dundrum was converted into a brand new Luas station. The old railway station building on the Taney Road side has been refurbished and now houses a café, but the station building on Main Street side had long been derelict, so it was demolished and a shelter erected in its place. Going in the city direction from Dundrum a brand new station was built at Windy Arbour, just off lower Churchtown Road.

BUS SERVICES TO DUNDRUM TOWN CENTRE

A total of seven Dublin Bus routes serve Dundrum Town Centre, while at the opposite end of Main Street there's a bus terminus close to the Luas station. One interesting regional bus service to Dundrum Town Centre is that provided by Kelly Travel, Limerick, which runs a twice weekly-service from Limerick, Roscrea and Nenagh to the Dundrum Town Centre and back again, for a return fare of €20. Dublin Bus has five direct services serving Dundrum itself.

44B Bus

Of all the bus routes serving Dundrum, none offers such a picturesque route as the 44B, which starts and terminates at the bus terminus beside the Dundrum Luas station. It started in the early 1930s, running as a Saturday service to and from D'Olier Street for shoppers coming into town from Glencullen. There was also a church bus on Sundays running from Eglinton Road in Donnybrook to Glecullen. A daily 44B bus service was started in the late 1940s and the bus still runs six days a week.

48A Bus

The first local bus service was introduced by the Dublin United Tramways Company and it linked Dundrum with D'Olier Street in the city centre by a very circuitous route, designed to avoid competing with the trams. Its route on the southside of Dublin city included Pearse Street, Westland Row, Merrion Square, Fitzwilliam Street, Leeson Street and Sallymount Avenue in Ranelagh. This bus service, the 48, ran every hour on the hour, but wasn't popular, so the 48A route was brought in, travelling every half hour via St Stephen's Green and Harcourt Street. Eventually, after these services had started in the late 1930s, the Sallymount Avenue route was abolished and all buses to and from Dundrum ran via St Stephen's Green, similar to the present-day Luas, which has its terminus on the Green. The 48A service was later allocated to the Goatstown service, which terminated opposite the Goat pub, but it was later extended to Kilmacud under route number 62. The 48A route had begun during the early 1930s, then in December 1937, came a major new expansion, double decker buses, which were introduced to the route by the Dublin United Tramway Company. But until the early 1950s, by which time the buses were being operated by Córas Iompair Éireann (CIÉ), the route still only ran as far as the crossroads in Dundrum. Then it was extended to reach what was then small settlement of Ballinteer, consisting mostly of rural cottages.

DONKEY CARTS

These were used in the Dundrum area until about seventy years ago. One photograph taken then shows some of the Richardson family, who lived in Main Street, in a cart with a near neighbour, Mary Mulvey, of the hardware shop and builders' providers.

DRUMM TRAIN

The Drumm battery train was the invention of Dr James Drumm, who was based at University College Dublin. Beneath the carriages of the train, huge batteries provided the motive power. The first Drumm train came into service on the line from Connolly station to Bray in 1932, but in subsequent years, Drumm trains were frequently used on the line from Harcourt Street to Bray, passing through Dundrum. In fact, the last Drumm train in service ran on this line on 12 July 1949. The battery-operated trains were charged at each end of the line and the trains worked very efficiently. During the fuel shortages of the Second World War, they were especially useful, but after the war, getting spare parts became increasingly difficult. But this unique Irish invention was a worthy predecessor of the Luas trams that run through Dundrum station today.

DUNDRUM BYPASS

The bypass, which runs from the big junction beneath the Dargan Luas bridge as far as Wyckham Way, was opened in 2002. It runs for a mere 1.2 kilometres and cost a staggering €44.4 million to build.

DUNDRUM'S ORIGINAL COACH SERVICES

Long before the railway was built from the city centre to Dundrum, people used horse-drawn coaches. This service ran from 1816 for a number of years. The charge for travelling inside the coach was one shilling and threepence for a single journey, while if passengers remained on the outside, the charge was tenpence. The service was started by a man called Robert Turbett and he did well from the new service, clearing a profit of £300 a year.

His plan was for a morning coach service from Dublin to Enniskerry, returning the same evening. The idea was that the morning coach would be filled by people going to Dundrum to breathe in the pure country air and drink goat's whey, as well as by sightseers going to see the Dargle waterfall. Turbett also organised a morning coach from Dundrum to Dublin, so that it would be filled by people living in Dundrum going to Dublin on business.

OLD RAILWAY BRIDGE

The bridge at Dundrum on the old Harcourt Street line lasted until the summer of 1960, although services on the line had ended on 1 January 1959. The bridge spanned a then narrow crossing at the junction of Taney Road and Dundrum Road. After the bridge was removed, the embankments were cut away, which is one of the reasons why the Dargan Luas bridge has to span such a wide junction.

But in the years immediately before the old bridge was demolished, tragedy had struck. On one occasion in the late 1950s, when the old bridge was being painted, a CIÉ workman was up ladders painting the underneath of the bridge when he slipped and fell, hitting his head on the street, which killed him instantly. Eyewitnesses who saw the accident said that the owner of nearby Conaty's butcher's shop came out, saw what had happened and threw his apron over the deceased CIÉ worker.

PUBLIC LIGHTING

These days, public lighting in the streets is taken for granted, but a century ago, Dundrum had none. After dark, Main Street was pitch black, with just a little weak light, mainly from oil lamps, coming from the shop windows. Paraffin oil was the method used for lighting houses and shops and Saunders hardware shop – where Mulveys pharmacy is now located – did a roaring trade in selling paraffin to people to refuel their lamps. Around 1910 two gas lamps were erected, one at each end of Main Street.

It wasn't until 1920 that gas lamps became more plentiful, in such locations as outside the police barracks on Upper Kilmacud Road, outside Deveney's, outside the library and on the bend of the road opposite St Nahi's church. The lamps had to be manually lit and extinguished by a lamplighter with a long pole, who travelled around by bicycle.

THOS. SAUNDERS, MAIN ST., DUNDRUM.

HAS TWO LARGE ESTABLISHMENTS WELL STOCKED.

They contain **General Drapery, Boots and Shoes, &c.**

Also a well-assorted Stock of **Ironmongery, Beds, and Bedding.**

GUARANTEED AT CITY PRICES.

THE HARCOURT STREET LINE

In 1846 two rival railway companies vied to provide routes from Dublin to Bray. The Dublin and Kingstown Railway, which had been opened in 1834 as the world's first commuter line, wanted to extend its line to Dalkey and Bray, which did in fact happen. It was also planned to build an inland line from Dublin to Bray. Two separate companies were involved in these schemes, the Dublin, Dundrum and Rathfarnham Railway and the Waterford, Wexford, Wicklow and Dublin Railway. The plan was that their routes would meet in Dundrum, but in the event, the Dublin and Wicklow Railway built the line from Dundrum to Bray and then took over the other company's line from Dundrum to Dublin. In Dublin, a temporary terminus was built at Harcourt Road, which opened in 1854. The railway was subsequently extended to the newly constructed station at the corner of Harcourt Street and Harcourt Road and this opened in 1859.

After passing across the spectacular Nine Arches viaduct in Milltown, still in place today, the line went south towards an embankment that ended with a short bridge across the junction of Dundrum Road and Taney Road, the site of the present-day Dargan Luas bridge. A little south of this bridge what was to become one of the busiest stations on the line was constructed, Dundrum station. Five kilometres from Harcourt Street, the station had access from both Main Street in Dundrum and from Taney Road.

As for the Nine Arches viaduct, if you look carefully today, you can still see the holes that were drilled in the base of its pillars during the Second World War, so that in the event of a British or German invasion of Ireland, explosives could be placed in position and the bridge blown up.

The station at Dundrum had originally been planned as the terminus of the line, so on the Taney Road side of the line an impressive mid-Victorian style single-storey building was constructed. It still stands today and is used as a café. But between the time the Harcourt Street railway was closed and the Luas was opened, this building was used for a variety of purposes. At one stage, Carr Communications, a public relations firm, had its headquarters there, with the celebrated public relations personality Terry Prone among its principals. The then head of the company, Bunny Carr, famed for his 'stop the lights' quiz show on RTÉ television, held forth in what had once been the old stationmaster's office. None other than the great railway pioneer himself, William Dargan, designed the station at Dundrum and had it constructed. In 1851 he had bought the house and farm at Mount Anville and he went on to become a director, then chairman, of the Dublin and Wicklow Railway. Dargan had a season ticket for the line and regularly used Dundrum station to get in and out of town, just like today's Luas commuters. For many years, up to the 1950s, the station was where boarding students at St Columba's College in Rathfarnham, 3 kilometres away, got off the train. The signal cabin on the Dublin platform had a large sign that read: 'Station for St Columba's College'. The sign was almost as large as the bilingual signs for the station itself.

The station was festooned with large enamel advertising signs, while it also had a variety of machines on the platform. One told people their weight, while another told their fortunes. Another machine embossed people's names on a strip of aluminium, twenty-two letters for one penny. Yet another machine invited people to test their strength; if they had great strength, their penny was returned. A further coin-operated machine dispensed bars of chocolate, toffee and chewing gum.

Up to the end of 1950s, the station served both Dundrum itself and the farmlands stretching as far as the Dublin Mountains. The station had a substantial passenger traffic and up until 1953 passengers could also travel south from Dundrum as far as Wexford, Rosslare and Waterford. Dundrum also had a substantial goods traffic and a goods siding was used extensively, including for milk vans belonging to O'Connor's Dairy, bagged cement for local builders and sometimes, horse boxes. It was also used for sending sugar beet grown on surrounding farms to the sugar factory in Carlow.

The last stationmaster at Dundrum, Andrew Smith, stated that very heavy goods traffic through Dundrum station continued right up until the end of the 1950s. Paul Campbell of Campbell's Shoe Repairs in Main Street recalls that if the family wanted to order supplies for their shop in those days, they'd send a postcard, with a halfpenny stamp, to the suppliers in Dublin city centre. Next day, the supplies would be sent out to Dundrum on an afternoon train, all very efficient.

Beyond Dundrum, the line entered a deep rock cutting and a rising gradient. In the closing days of 1957, two diesel railcars collided in this cutting. The accident happened in the dark about 6 p.m., on 23 December that year about 0.8 kilometres south of Dundrum station. A cow had been spotted on the track and a train from Bray was proceeding very slowly, because the cow couldn't be moved from the track in the deep cutting. The red tail lamp on this train wasn't working, because its oil hadn't been replenished in Bray. So the train coming up fast behind, also travelling from Bray, ploughed into the rear of the first train, at speed. The driver of this train, Andy Larkin, was killed and the guard on the first train and three of the twenty passengers on both trains were injured, but not seriously. Such was the damage that full train services on the line didn't resume until after Christmas.

Until the mid-1950s, when the Churchtown postal sorting office was opened, mail was sent regularly by train to Dundrum. When it was off-loaded it was taken on a mail cart, pushed by a postman from the station at Dundrum to the post office, which was situated where AIB bank is now located. Out-going mail was taken from the post office to the railway station by the same method. When the Churchtown office opened, to serve the postal needs of the entire Dublin 14 district, these quaint customs ceased.

One of the more unusual sights on the railway in Dundrum was the spectacle provided by the four-man maintenance gang, the platelayers, who were based at Dundrum station. They had a four-wheel bogey on which they transported all their equipment and often in the evenings, passengers at Dundrum saw the four men sitting on the bogey coming down the incline from Stillorgan, having finished their day's work.

Another amusing story was provided by a lady passenger who was travelling from Wexford to Dundrum. When she arrived there, she realised that she'd left her hat box on a platform seat in Wexford. The stationmaster promptly reassured her that the hat box would be put on the next available train. The next day, a horse box arrived at Dundrum station marked 'Urgent-Dundrum'.

In late 1954, diesel engines started taking over from the steam engines that had previously worked the route. The only previous exception to steam had been between 1939 and 1949 when the line was worked largely by Drumm battery trains (see page 120). After June 1957 the Harcourt Street line was worked exclusively by diesel engines, but their use didn't alleviate the heavy losses the lines was making, partly because of competition from bus services. At the end of October 1958, CIÉ announced that the Harcourt Street line would close as from 1 January 1959. The passenger traffic on the line was about 1,000 a day and freight traffic was minimal. As a result of the closure, seventy-four railway workers lost their jobs.

After the line was closed down, the tracks were removed and by June of 1960, all the track had been lifted as far as Foxrock. That same year also saw the railway bridge at Dundrum being demolished. The first murmurings about the need to reopen the line started emerging in 1969 but it took forty years from the closure of the old line for the decision to be made to resurrect it in the form of a Luas tram line.

THE DUNDRUM LUAS BRIDGE

The new Dargan Luas bridge, one of the most spectacular in Ireland, dates back to 2001 when work began, forty-nine years after the old Harcourt Street line had closed. The bridge was designed by Roughan O'Donovan, which had begun its design work in 1996. Two contracts were issued for the new bridge, one for the foundations, and the other for the actual bridge. Altogether the bridge took eighteen months to complete.

After the foundations were laid work began on the huge concrete pylon, 50 metres high, which holds the cable stays on the bridge. Then came the task of building the bridge itself across the huge road junction. Tony Dempsey, a director of Roughan O'Donovan, explained that a total of forty-three concrete segments for the deck of the bridge were cast in Northern Ireland. The main contractors for the bridge were Grahams. The whole span of the bridge is 180 metres. As each concrete segment was lifted into place, it was connected up to the cable stays and each segment was glued to the next segment using epoxy resin, which is far stronger than concrete itself.

When the segments were being put in place, the surrounding roads were closed at 8 p.m. each night, then the segments were lowered into place and linked up to the cable stays around midnight, with the roads reopening about five or six o'clock the following morning.

No daytime work was done on positioning the segments, so daytime traffic flows at Taney Cross junction were uninterrupted. This was the first bridge of its kind in Ireland and the inspiration for the bridge technology came from France. Before he joined Roughan & O'Donovan, which now utilises its Sandyford-based bridge-building technologies around the world, Tony Dempsey had worked in France, where cable stay technology had been pioneered. Some of the people he worked with there had worked on the Pont de Normandie across the Seine estuary near Le Havre. That bridge is 800 metres long and the longest cable stay bridge in the world. Very similar technology to that used on the Dundrum bridge is being used on the new bridge being built at New Ross, County Wexford.

Even though the Dargan Luas bridge in Dundrum was completed near the end of 2002, it took another two-and-a-half years before

Luas trains started using the bridge, when the Luas Green line opened on 30 June 2004. Three weeks later, on 19 July 2004, the bridge was officially named by the then Transport Minister Seamus Brennan, also a local TD, as the William J. Dargan Bridge after the great railway pioneer. The operating company for the Luas system became Veolia Transport Ireland. In October 2010, the Green line was extended by 11 kilometres to Bride's Glen and in recent years, the frequency of trams on the line has been stepped up. It's unclear when, if ever, the line will be extended beyond Bride's Glen so that passengers can continue through to Bray.

WICKLOW HILLS BUS COMPANY

Some of the earliest buses to run on what is now the 44 bus route from Dublin to Enniskerry, via Dundrum, were operated by the Residents' Bus Company. This had been organised in the 1920s by the residents of Enniskerry, when enough money was collected to buy a secondhand Renault 16 bus. Business was so brisk that soon a second Renault coach, this time a twenty-seater, was bought.

But the Residents' Bus Company gave way in the mid-1920s to another bus company, the Wicklow Hills Bus Company, based in Enniskerry. Its service started in St Stephen's Green and went via Dundrum village to Enniskerry. The Wicklow Hills bus firm was started by a businessman from Mullingar called Thomas Fitzpatrick, who lived in Bray. The headquarters of the company was in Enniskerry, where all its buses were garaged. The new company started off well and its services proved popular, even though its buses lacked modern-day amenities and the tyres on its buses were solid, which made for bumpy rides. Drivers were comparatively well paid at £3 10s a week.

In March 1927, not long after the service had started, a cyclist from Rathfarnham called Peter Young was killed when he and his bicycle were in collision with a Wicklow Hills bus in the centre of Dundrum. At the local district court in Dundrum, in July 1928, District Justice Reddin accused buses from the Wicklow Hills Bus Company and those from the rival Robin bus firm of racing one another on the Enniskerry road near Balally.

In the 1920s and early 1930s some of the bus services in Dublin were run by the tram company and others by a variety of private operators. At one stage the tramway company introduced buses in the Dundrum area with the express purpose of driving away the competition from the Robin buses and the tramway's company bus, nicknamed locally as 'the Robin Chaser' had the desired effect.

The writing on the wall for the Wicklow Hills Bus Company, indeed for all private bus companies, came in 1933 when the Road Transport Act gave the Dublin United Tramways company powers to purchase its private sector competitors.

Thomas Fitzpatrick fought tooth and nail to keep his buses going, but in the end, he had to admit defeat. At Easter 1936 its services ceased, on the takeover of the company by the Dublin Tram Company, which promptly created the 44 bus route. Nine years later, in 1945, when CIÉ was formed, the Dublin United Tramways Company was nationalised, along with the Great Southern Railway. In 1987 CIÉ was split up into various operating divisions, including Dublin Bus, but the 44 bus route has kept the same number to this day.

13

WORK

BANK OF IRELAND

The Bank of Ireland premises in Main Street, close to the entrance to the Luas station, stands on an historically interesting site. A pub was once located there, firstly called Hilliards and then named after Andy Murtagh. The pub later gave way to a boot and shoe repairing business run by Charlie Hanlon. Then the premises became a chemist's, first Hayes & Hayes, then Carvilles. The new Bank of Ireland building opened in March 1981. It had been built by the contracting firm owned by Jim Clarke, who still lives on Dundrum's Main Street.

CUALA PRESS

This was one of the earliest artistic endeavours set up in the area, back in 1902.

John Butler Yeats, father of W.B. Yeats, had spent many years in England but returned to Ireland in 1902 with his two daughters to take up residence in Churchtown. The house they were going to live in when they arrived wasn't ready, so they took up temporary accommodation in Sydenham Villas, where they stayed for some months.

John Butler Yeats's two daughters, Susan Mary (Lily) and Elizabeth Corbett (Lolly), together with Evelyn Gleeson and Gracie McCormack, wanted to start a handcraft enterprise making hand-tufted carpets, tapestries, embroideries, hand-printed books and broadsides. Both sisters had previous experience with the renowned English wallpaper designer and manufacturer, William Morris.

They rented a house called Runnymede, on Sandyford Road, a short distance from Dundrum, and changed the name of the house to Dun Emer, after the wife of Cúchulainn, who was herself skilled in embroidery, and started the Dun Emer Guild. Five years after the start of this craft-making enterprise, Lily, together with her father, went to the Great New York Exhibition in 1907 to demonstrate their carpet weaving and tapestry weaving skills. Miss Pollexfen, a relative of the Yeats family, showed the embroidery side of the work. Much younger than the Yeats sisters, she lived with them at what became their permanent home in Churchtown, Gurteen Dheas. Lily Yeats wanted to expand the hand-printing side of the business, so she acquired a four-bedroomed cottage near their Churchtown home, renamed it Cuala and created the Cuala Press.

Dun Emer Industries ran the Cuala Press and produced embroidery. The rest of their activities had already been hived off into a separate company, the Dun Emer Guild Ltd, run by Evelyn Gleeson. The creation of the two separate organisations was the result of deep-seated personality differences in the original organisation.

At the Cuala Press, illustrations by Jack B. Yeats, brother of W.B. Yeats, were often used in its books. The last book the Cuala Press published came out in 1946 and in 1986 the Cuala Press archives were donated to Trinity College, Dublin, by Michael and Gráinne Yeats, children of W.B. Yeats.

The embroidery, tapestry and hand-printing divisions were known locally as the 'Industry'. The work from Dun Emer Guild found its way all over the world, even as far as Government House in Canberra, Australia. Carpets were supplied to such distinguished residences as Áras an Uachtaráin and in 1932, during the Eucharistic Congress in Dublin, a Dun Emer carpet was presented to the then Pope.

One local person who was closely connected with the 'Industry' for most of her life was Sara Hyland, born at Main Street in 1893, and who died in 1972. She was renowned, famous even, for the quality of her embroidery. Sara subsequently became blind, but following an operation, she regained her sight. Among her many skills, she was an Irish language enthusiast, closely involved with the local Conradh na Gaeilge branch. She also taught embroidery at the local 'tech' and later in life, became assistant librarian at the Carnegie Library in Dundrum, helping the long-time librarian, May Courtney, who also worked in the 'Industry'. Sara wrote a long text called 'My Story', covering eight periods of her life, from 1893 to 1933, but she failed to get it published, since it was considered 'too local'.

Lily and Lolly Yeats, were both buried at St Nahi's in Dundrum, as was Grainne Yeats.

However, in developing the heritage of Dundrum, a frequently heard complaint is that the area has never capitalised on its connections with the Yeats family.

DAVE'S BOOK WAREHOUSE

Dave Downes, a well-known trader in antiquarian and old books, had a close association with the Dundrum area for many years, running his business from a warehouse by the old railway station from 1996 to 2000, and then for a couple of years at Gort Muire. The business is now located in Stillorgan. Dave says that at one stage in Dundrum he had a big problem with local delinquents and drug addicts, especially in spring and summer, when they would gather in front of the smaller building on the site, the front of which looked out over the Dundrum Road-Taney Road crossroads. Today, that crossroads is beneath the Dargan Luas bridge. Dave had a number of break-ins at his Dundrum premises, but he says that thieves never stole any books.

DUNDRUM BUSINESS PARK

Among the offices located here on Dundrum Road is the Dundrum office of Dún Laoghaire-Rathdown County Council, which provides the full range of county council services to the Dundrum area. The building was acquired towards the end of 1994 when the new county council was being formed. The building was officially opened in September 1995. It offers a public counter service for residents of the area and office staff are responsible for maintaining and publishing the Register of Electors for the entire county. The building is also used for meetings, including those with local residents' associations and it also has a small exhibition space.

The old Dublin County Council used to have its local offices just off Main Street in Dundrum, close to the railway line.

DUNDRUM CREDIT UNION

This South Dublin Credit Union was founded in 1966, ten years after the first Irish credit union had been established in Dún Laoghaire. When the credit union started in Dundrum its assets were slight, barely amounting to £1. Today its assets are worth over €80 million. The credit union began in a makeshift office at the Carnegie Library and this was open just one night a week, on Fridays. In 1986, it moved to Pembroke Lodge on Main Street, which it had bought from the Richardson family. For a number of years, they used the old house but then decided to build an extension at the back. Then they discovered that the front of the house had lots of leaks, so that was rebuilt as well. Eventually, the whole premises were demolished and rebuilt and that fine purpose-built centre still operates on Main Street. In addition to its head office in Dundrum, the credit union has branches at Ballinteer, Rathfarnham and Knocklyon, while it also has a branch at Belfield (UCD). Altogether, about thirty people work for this credit union, divided about half and half between full-time and part-time workers.

HARMONIA PUBLISHING

This publishing company, possibly the largest magazine publishers in Ireland, is based at Rosemount on the Dublin side of Dundrum. It produces about 2.2 million magazine copies a year.

Harmonia was founded by a former nurse, Norah Casey, and publishes women's magazines as well as other titles such as *Ireland of the Welcomes*. It also publishes much material on the internet. About ten years ago, the company moved from Clanwilliam House, at Mount Street Bridge, to Dundrum. In October 2013 Norah Casey stepped down as CEO of the company and other members of her family, including her younger brother Ciaran, became responsible for running the company. Norah Casey's husband, Richard Hannaford, a former BBC health correspondent, had died tragically young in 2011. He too was very involved in Harmonia. With the departure of the *Irish Daily Star* from Dundrum, Harmonia is now the only major magazine publisher in the area, but Norah Casey is now concentrating on her TV and radio career.

At the start of the twenty-first century, a lively magazine called *Suburb*, edited by Maxine Jones, covered much of south Dublin, including Dundrum. It was published from 2001 to 2002.

ILFORD PHOTOGRAPHIC

Until the late 1980s, Dundrum Castle House was a popular rendezvous for anyone connected with the photographic trade. Ilford Ireland, then a leading supplier of photographic film and equipment for photographers, was based at Dundrum Castle House.

IRISH DAILY STAR

The *Irish Daily Star* had its office in the Dundrum Town Centre, from 2010 until 2013. Before that, it has been based in Terenure. The paper was started in 1988 as a joint venture between what was then Independent Newspapers and the Daily Express group in the UK. A Sunday version was launched in 2003, but because of declining sales, it was closed a year after the operation moved to Dundrum. The daily paper continues, but like virtually every other newspaper in Ireland, it has lost substantial sales and now sells around 55,000 copies a day. At the start of 2013, Independent News & Media took full executive responsibility for the *Irish Daily Star,* closed the Dundrum office and moved it to its main Dublin office in Talbot Street.

Much earlier, in the 1980s, Southside Publishing, which produced freesheets, was based at Dundrum Castle House. Today, freesheets in the area include the *Dundrum Informer*, bi-monthly, and the *Dundrum Gazette*, a weekly.

MANOR MILL LAUNDRY

For many years, from 1864 until 1942, when it closed down, the Manor Mill Laundry was the main employer in the Dundrum area, with several hundred people, mostly female, working for it. The Manor Mill was one of the largest laundry concerns in the Dublin area, which had about twenty competitors, including a couple attached to convents. Its competitors included such other renowned laundry names as the White Heather, the White Swan, the Kelso and the Swastika, as well as the Model Steam Laundry in Ballyboden.

The Edmundsons, a Quaker family, were behind the Dundrum laundry as well as the old laundry at Milltown, whose chimney can still be seen today beside the Seven Arches bridge on the Luas Green line.

In Dundrum, the Manor Mill dated back to the fifteenth century and it was used for over three centuries to grind corn for local farmers. The River Slang was used to power the mill and after the Edmundsons took over the derelict buildings they turned them into the laundry. Water from the river had long been diverted from the River Slang to form the millpond and the overflow water from the pond was used eventually by the laundry to generate its own electricity, making the Manor Mill Laundry green long before its time!

The present-day version of the laundry pond can still be seen as a feature of the Dundrum Town Centre. Clothes were washed in the laundry's very large washroom before being carefully dried in huge centrifugal driers. The washerwomen had to work in their bare feet, as the water spilled out over the floor, although in later years, the washing process was mechanised. Sometimes, if the weather was fine, clothes were hung out to dry. The original laundry building

was single-storied, but in later years, an extension was built, facing Ballinteer Road, that was used for ironing clothes.

Collecting dirty washing for the laundry was a complex affair, as the laundry's business area extended over much of south County Dublin and County Wicklow. Most of the incoming laundry was collected by horse-drawn vans, and then by motorised vans when these became available in the early twentieth century. Every article that came into the laundry had its own indelible mark, so that it could be easily traced.

Larger customers had their own wicker work baskets, which were also marked, but with black paint. An advertisement in *The Irish Times* in 1917 described the Manor Mill Laundry as having a beautiful country situation in County Dublin. Its setting was only rivalled by the excellence of its work. Shirts and collars were superbly finished, while washing to be delivered by rail and post was specially quoted for.

Work at the laundry began at 8 a.m. and before that, the hooter sounded at 7.50 a.m., continuing for about thirty seconds. The final short blast on the hooter came precisely on the dot of 8 a.m. and it was the signal for work to start inside the laundry. The hooter also sounded at 2 p.m. when it was time for the workers to return to work after their lunch break, then called a dinner break. During that break, many of the workers went just down the road into Main Street, to the shops, so the laundry's workers were an invaluable source of income for local traders. Up until the late 1930s the laundry hooter, the Angelus bells and Sunday Mass bells at Holy Cross church in Main Street provided all the timekeeping that many people in Dundrum needed.

Working conditions at the laundry were tough and on one occasion in the 1920s the female workers went on strike for fifteen weeks. When it was settled, they got two weeks paid holiday a year, almost unheard of at the time. The local representative of the Irish Women Workers' Union was Mrs Sarah Kennedy, who lived at 20 Pembroke Cottages. She also organised the first ever annual workers' excursion from the laundry, a day trip to Glendalough.

During the later 1930s the laundry invested in more mechanisation, but the advent of the Second World War, with all its shortages, put pay to the business. The shortages of cleaning materials and fuel, as well as continuing labour troubles in the laundry, resulted in it closing down for good in 1942. One of the other laundries that benefitted from the closure was the Dartry Dye Works, just beyond Milltown, which had two agents in Dundrum. One agency was at the old post office at 8 Main Street, while the other was held by a man called McKnight who lived in Ashgrove Terrace.

After the laundry closed in 1942, its premises became the Pye factory, while other light industries were also located there.

MCGRANE'S DAIRY

Until around sixty years ago, McGrane's Balally Dairy on Sandyford Road was a hive of activity, a family business run by the McGranes. Edward McGrane, the owner, had married three times and had close to a dozen children, who often helped out in the dairy. His three sons, Bill, Edward and John, all helped out on the farm, while the womenfolk, besides looking after all the domestic chores in the farmhouses, also helped prepare and deliver the milk. None of the McGrane family was ever known to take a holiday, as this was a seven days a week operation, running both the dairy and the farm. But while the McGranes dairy and farm was for long in almost open country, by the 1960s housing estates were starting to encroach and these days, what were once extensive fields is now a vast suburban conglomeration.

McGrane's also had extensive farming activities, where the highlight was the threshing, at the conclusion of the late summer harvest. The steam loco and the wagon used for this were brought to the farm by contractors the previous evening. At 6 a.m. on the day of the threshing, the engine man got going and within two hours, he had steam up on the loco. Then the blades on the mill separated the wheat from the chaff and straw. The grains of barley and wheat were put into sacks, while the chaff and straw was used for cattle bedding. Threshing was really hard work and in addition to the three McGrane sons, casual labour from the district was employed and all day long, the women in the farmhouse kept an endless supply of beer, tea and sandwiches going, all prepared under the watchful eye of Mrs McGrane.

As for Mr McGrane, he was known both as 'The Boss' and 'Oul Neddy'. He was renowned for being short tempered, but he was always kind to children and frequently gave them a couple of pennies for running messages. While McGrane's was a well-known local dairy, it had a lot of competition from close on thirty other dairies either based in the Dundrum area or selling into it. Another locally based diary was Doyles, based at Frankfort Castle, while other familiar local names included Cosgraves, Farrellys, Fergusons, McCanns, Nolans, O'Connors Lakelands Dairy, the Overends at Airfield, Priestleys, Whitneys and Youngs. The Lambert family had two dairies, one run by Bob Lambert, the other by George Lambert. Hughes Brothers dairy absorbed nearly all these local dairies, but what was once Hughes

Brothers has long since been incorporated into Premier Dairies, itself part of the huge Glanbia operation. The only local dairying operation from this once vast field of local dairy companies, delivering fresh milk door to door, is that of the Jersey herd at Airfield.

MELLON'S GARAGE

Mellon's, which was once a leading business on Main Street in Dundrum, had quite a collection of characters working for it, but in the office, rather than in the garage itself, as the late John Mellon recalled. One was a retired Garda superintendent, who when he was dry, was as good as gold. But he had a habit of disappearing on 'benders' and on one occasion, disappeared to County Tipperary for two weeks before drying out and coming back to work. Another member of the office staff often disappeared during the day for lavatory breaks, which in fact were quick trips on the train to the bar in Harcourt Street station. Yet another of the heavy drinkers in Mellon's office was a retired major who had served in the British Army in the Far East during the Second World War.

NEW ISLAND BOOKS

Described as Ireland's leading publisher of ground-breaking fiction, New Ireland Books had started out in the 1980s as the Raven Arts Press, run by Dermot Bolger. For many years it was based in Brookside, Dundrum, but in 2014 it moved to new premises in Sandyford.

NOLAN'S FORGE

For many years, Dundrum had two forges, one beside what is now Campbell's Corner, the other on the Dundrum side of the old railway bridge. This was Nolan's forge, which following the decline in horse-drawn transport in the 1920s, went into steel fabrication. Nolan's forge was run by the father of the late Jim Nolan, an historian of Dundrum. Dundrum had a second forge, just at the start of Ballinteer Road, immediately behind the present-day Campbell's Corner.

Beside Nolan's forge, in a small entry, was a bookie's shop, known locally as 'Jack the Bookie'. Much of the business was done by agents or 'runners', while in the old days, bread van drivers often collected bets and delivered winnings on their routes. These bread van drivers took many other messages as well, including wet and dry radio batteries when they needed to be recharged.

OLD DUNDRUM MILLS

Water powered milling has been connected with the millpond on the River Slang, close to the present-day pond at the Dundrum Town Centre, since the early seventeenth century. The first reference to a watermill in Dundrum came in 1627. It's possible that over 1,000 years ago, the monastery at St Nahi's had a mill, but no evidence of this has been found. In the eighteenth century mills were still evident on the Slang River in Dundrum, while Windy Arbour also had a paper mill. In the early nineteenth century, what had once been a paper mill at Windy Arbour had become a silk throwing factory. But following the withdrawal of protection duties in 1826, the silk mill was turned into a starch mill, then a bark mill.

At Dundrum, the early mills ground corn, while by 1800, it was noted that Dundrum had two additional mills, one a paper mill, the other an iron mill. The 1837 Ordnance Survey map noted that at the Dundrum Ironworks, the majority of buildings, except three, were single storey and that most of them were thatched. But four buildings, including Mill House, were slated. By 1860, the ironworks was vacant, but by 1864, the laundry had started up on the site.

By 1849 there was no further evidence of milling in Windy Arbour. Milltown also had mills, including a flour and saw mills and when Gibney's mill closed about 1885, this was the end of milling on the Slang.

PYE WORKS

For many years, the Pye works in Dundrum, where the Dundrum Town Centre is now located, was the main employer, with 1,200 people on its payroll, mostly female. Pye was an English firm that was in at the start of radio broadcasts in England, at the beginning of the 1920s. A young man from Cappoquin, west Waterford, called C.O. Stanley, took it over soon afterwards.

In London, he had made his way with little experience and even less money, but managed to buy out Pye and turn it into a thriving concern. At its peak, Pye in England employed 36,000 people and its smaller Irish factory was also a thriving employer, but on a much smaller scale.

Pye had started in Dublin as an agency, operating out of the Corn Exchange building on Burgh Quay in the mid-1930s, controlled by J.P. Digby. Imported radio sets attracted heavy import duty, so he started a manufacturing operation in 1937 at Temple Lane in the city centre. This prospered, so much so that in 1943 it moved to much larger premises, in what had been the Manor Mill Laundry in Dundrum, which had closed down the year previously.

About fifteen years later, Pye Ireland built a brand new factory, slightly out of Dundrum, off Sandyford Road. Pye made a name for itself with its radio sets and these were the early mainstay of the Dundrum factory, along with radiograms and gramophones. But Stanley was also a keen advocate of independent commercial television, which started in Britain in 1955, so the company soon became renowned for its television sets. After the Irish television service, Telefís Éireann started on the last day of December 1961, Pye Ireland had acquired a brand new market.

By that stage, Pye was assembling and marketing 19-inch and 23-inch television sets, on 405 and 625 lines, as well as portable radio sets and transistorised radio sets for cars. It also did record players and a new wonder, radiograms that produced stereo sound, a real novelty for the time.

Someone who worked briefly at Pye, at the start of his career, sixty years ago, was the late Albert Reynolds, a former Taoiseach. When he joined, he said that he had been in a union at a small factory in Longford, but as soon as the union bosses in the highly unionised factory found this wasn't the case, Albert Reynolds had to leave the job hurriedly. He'd been taken on as a polisher of radio sets, for the grand sum of £26 week.

Besides assembling television and radio sets, the Dundrum factory assembled many other kinds of electrical products, including refrigerators, even oil heaters and motor bikes from Czechoslovakia. The Pye record label was renowned. For many years, the factory was run by managing director J.P. Digby and then his son Dr Liam Dillon Digby. At the end of the Pye era in Dundrum, the company was being run by a man called Price.

However, in 1966 Pye found itself seriously over-extended and C.O. Stanley and his son John were ousted from the company. Within a decade, Pye had been completely taken over by Philips. John was laden with most of the blame for the debacle, rather than his father.

In the last two decades of its existence, Pye Ireland diversified significantly, as it couldn't balance its books simply on the basis of the radio and TV sets it was assembling. In its latter days, the firm obtained a large Middle Eastern contract, which necessitated the building of a new factory. A combination of bad weather and a strike at the Irish cement works meant that construction was delayed and the Middle Eastern contract was lost. What was to have been the new Pye factory was turned into a supermarket, first for H. Williams and then for Quinnsworth and Crazy Prices.

Eventually, in 1980, Pye sold Mill House, close to its original Dundrum factory, to Jean Dillon, wife of the original managing director and mother of Dr Liam Dillon Digby.

The factory, however, managed to carry on until 1985, when it closed down. At the height of its production, it had employed 550 men and 650 women on assembly work. After the closure, the premises were utilised for other activities, such as the Dundrum Bowl, but eventually, what became known as the Pye lands, were used for the construction of the Dundrum Town Centre.

RSA

Immediately south of Dundrum Town Centre, the Royal Sun Alliance (RSA) insurance group, one of the largest operating in Ireland, has its headquarters, employing about 850 people. It has been providing insurance cover in Ireland since 1721.

SCHOOL AND COLLEGE PUBLISHING

One well-known firm in the area in the 1990s was School and College Publishing, at the junction of Taney Road and Dundrum Road. It remained in the old station building until the building of the Luas line started fifteen years ago.

WINDY ARBOUR VILLAGE ASSOCIATION

This association has been active in recent years in promoting the development of Windy Arbour and its businesses, including Ireland's first certified organic shop, Ecologic, which was set up about fifteen years ago. Shan Kelly is the energetic spokesperson for the group, which is constantly promoting improvements to the district. It had been mooted in 2011, then the following year, it started up, with about thirty member firms and organisations, including some in the Dundrum Business Park.

TELEPHONE EXCHANGE

As early as 1892, residents in Dundrum could be connected by telephone. The Telephone Company of Ireland had a franchise at Edward Doyle's grocery shop on Main Street.

For many years, the manual exchange was located at 3 Main Street and run by Mrs Gorman. This exchange pre-dated the First World War. It was blown up during the War of Independence, and then rebuilt.

In earlier days, phone numbers in Dundrum didn't run to more than two digits (the Manor Mill Laundry was Dundrum 7) but as the system was modernised and numbers became much longer, many telephone subscribers in the Dundrum area still retained their original two digit numbers, included in their new numbers. A major step forward came in 1953, when the telephone exchange was automated.

FURTHER READING

Íde Ní Riain, *A History of Mount Anville, 1790-1988* (privately published, Dublin, 1988)

Peter Pearson, *Between the Mountains and the Sea* (Dublin, 1998)

Patrick Mellon, *Dundrum Boy* (privately published, County Wexford, 2008)

Brian MacAonghusa, *Luas Harcourt Street Memories* (Dublin, 2004)

Patrick Geoghegan, *Robert Emmet, a Life* (Dublin, 2002)

Jim Nolan, *The Changing Face of Dundrum* (Dublin, 1981)

F. Elrington Ball, *The Parish of Taney* (Dublin, 1895)

Kevin Harrington, *The Way to Dundrum* (privately published, Dublin, 1988)

Carol Robinson, *Taney, Portrait of a Parish* (Tweed, Dublin, 1994)

If you enjoyed this book, you may also be interested in…

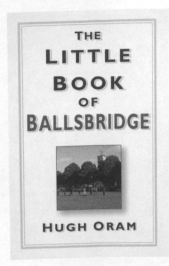

The Little Book of Ballsbridge

HUGH ORAM

This is a compendium of fascinating, obscure, strange and entertaining facts about this leafy suburb of Dublin.

Here you will find out about Ballsbridge's famous (and occasionally infamous) residents, its proud sporting heritage, its churches and great houses and its natural history. Down wide streets and past elegant houses, this book takes the reader on a journey through Ballsbridge and its vibrant past.

A reliable reference book and a quirky guide, this can be dipped into time and time again to reveal something new about the people, the heritage and the secrets of Dublin's 'embassy belt'.

978 1 84588 812 1

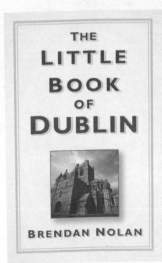

The Little Book of Dublin

BRENDAN NOLAN

This is a compendium of fascinating and entertaining truths about the city, past and present.

Funny, fast-paced and fact-packed, here you will discover Dublin's trade and industry, saints and sinners, crime and punishment, sports and games, folklore and customs and, of course, its literary heritage. Here lie famous elements of Dublin's history cheek by jowl with little-known facts that could so easily pass unnoticed.

This treasure trove can be dipped into time and time again to revealsomething new about this ancient and beautiful city.

978 1 84588 815 2